W9-AAJ-207

Being God's Partner

How to Find the Hidden Link

Between Spirituality and Your Work

Jeffrey K. Salkin

With an Introduction by Norman Lear

Jewish Lights Publishing
Woodstock, Vermont

Being God's Partner:
How to Find the Hidden Link Between Spirituality and Your Work

Library of Congress Cataloging-in-Publication Data

Salkin, Jeffrey K., 1954 –
Being God's partner :
how to find the hidden link between spirituality and your work /
by Jeffrey K. Salkin.
p. cm.
Includes bibliographical references.
ISBN 1-879045-37-0 (hardcover)
1. Spiritual life—Judaism.
2. Work—Religious aspects—Judaism.
3. Judaism and labor.
4. Business ethics.
5. Ethics, Jewish.
I. Title.
BM723.S243 1994 94 – 29471
296.7'4—dc20 CIP

First edition
10 9 8 7 6 5 4 3 2 1
Manufactured in the United States of America

Book and cover designed by Glenn Suokko

Published by Jewish Lights Publishing
A Division of LongHill Partners Inc.
PO Box 237
Sunset Farm Offices, Route 4
Woodstock, Vermont 05091
Tel: 802 457-4000 Fax: 802 457-4004

Also by Jeffrey K. Salkin

Putting God on the Guest List:
How to Reclaim the Spiritual Meaning
of Your Child's Bar or Bat Mitzvah

(Jewish Lights Publishing)

To Nina, Samuel, and Gabriel,
who have taught me that "husband" and "father"
is a wonderful job title.

To Brenda Gevertz, Lee Friedlander,
Marc and Betty Gellman, Marcia Kramer, Joy Levitt,
Egon Mayer, Carl Rheins, Richard and Jeannie Siegel,
for making Shabbat Shabbat.

Being God's Partner

How to Find the Hidden Link Between Spirituality and Your Work

Contents

Acknowledgments

I wrote *Being God's Partner: How to Find the Hidden Link Between Spirituality and Your Work* with the hopes of articulating a Jewish theology of the workplace, as well as a new way of thinking about Judaism and spirituality. I wanted Jews (and others) to think about how God can enter what many dismiss as the most mundane aspect of our lives — our work.

That vision found sustenance from several sources. I thank my publisher, Stuart Matlins of Jewish Lights Publishing. In the past several years, Stuart has become more than simply a publisher. He has become a fellow traveler on the journey, a visionary about Jewish books that will not only stimulate the mind, but refresh the soul. More than that, he has become a good friend, and a role model for what it means to have an engaged Jewish heart.

I am grateful, also, to my editor, Arthur Magida. Arthur went above and beyond the call of duty more times than I can count. I am grateful for much: His skilled eye and perceptive command of style and usage; his quick mind blessed with the ability to cut through the jargon and get to the heart of the matter; and his sensitive ability to rouse my spirits when they were flagging. He never lost faith in this project. I am ever in his debt.

I learned much from the people with whom I spoke and whose stories are recorded in the book. They are too many to name, and they form a diverse group: Congregants (though I have not used any confidential material, or anything that emerged from a counselling session), old and new friends, college roommates, colleagues, and plain ordinary Jews and non-Jews. I am especially grateful to Don Scharf, Certified Social Worker, for his insights into the inner world of the workaholic. They have all taught me that our individual stories are a Torah that is still being written, and which needs to be expounded.

A word needs to be said in tribute to my congregants at Central Synagogue of Nassau County, Rockville Centre, New York. They have always encouraged me to take learning and teaching seriously. Much of what is in these pages emerged from classes, workshops, and sermons I gave at Central. My congregants' insights about themselves and their work have truly inspired me and provided much grist for the mill that produced this book. My secretary, Peggy Tompkins, took an active role in some of the nitty-gritty administrative details surrounding the final stages of this manuscript. Her cheerful support has been much appreciated.

Acharon acharon haviv, the best for last: My wife, Nina Rubin Salkin. Her support, encouragement, nurturance, and enthusiasm for the task was always apparent. To my sons, Samuel and Gabriel, whose presence I missed as I, ironically, was writing about workaholism, I am grateful.

I give thanks to You, O Holy One of Being, for sending me teachers to teach me, and students to learn from me, and for helping me find inspiration and humility even — and especially — in the ordinary moments of life.

Jeffrey K. Salkin
Rockville Centre, New York
June 15, 1994

Preface

Occasionally, I'm asked where the idea for this book came from. The idea was born on the day, seven years ago, when we moved from Doylestown, Pennsylvania to Rockville Centre. The boss of the moving crew was a delightful, crusty gentleman, a dead ringer for Willie Nelson. I had never met anyone so enthusiastic about his or her work, and I asked him the source of that enthusiasm.

"Well, you see, I'm a religious man," he answered, "and my work is part of my religious mission."

"What do you mean?" I asked.

"Well, it's like this. Moving is hard for most people. It's a very vulnerable time for them. People are nervous about going to a new community, and about having strangers pack their most precious possessions. So, I think God wants me to treat my customers with love and to make them feel that I care about their things and their life. God wants me to help make their changes go smoothly. If I can be happy about it, maybe they can be, too."

I forgot his name long ago. But, like so many anonymous people, he was a messenger of God. He was the first lay person I ever met who believed that God wanted him to do his job in a certain way, and that his work was part of his religious orientation to the world.

It is not surprising that this gentleman was a pious Christian since Christians have thought more than Jews about work and spirituality. Christians are very comfortable speaking about "vocation"; Jews, much less so. As the Christian author, Frederick Buechner, wrote in *Wishful Thinking: A Theological ABC:*

> "...The kind of work God usually calls you to is the kind of work (a) that you need most to do and (b) the world most needs to have done. If you really get a kick out of your work, you've presumably met requirement (a), but if your work is writing TV deodorant commercials, the chances are you've missed requirement (b). On the other hand, if your work is being a doctor in a leper colony, you have probably met (b), but if most of the time you're bored and depressed by it, the chances are you haven't only bypassed (a) but probably aren't helping your patients much either....The place God calls you to is the place where your deep gladness and the world's deep hunger meet."

The seminal work on the sociological relationship between religion and work is Max Weber's *The Protestant Ethic and The Spirit of Capitalism.* No Jew has written a book that corresponds to Weber's. I am indebted, therefore, to those Christian writers and thinkers who have paved the way for me to discover the spiritual nature of work.

Several years ago, I wrote *Putting God on the Guest List: How to Reclaim the Spiritual Meaning of Your Child's Bar or Bat Mitzvah* (Jewish Lights Publishing, 1992). It was about one of the most often-discussed topics in American Jewish culture — bar and bat mitzvah — and how Jews can reinvigorate those ceremonies with deep spiritual meaning.

I knew there was a need for the message of *Putting God on the Guest List,* but I never anticipated the strength of the response to it. The reaction to *Putting God on the Guest List* emphasized for me the spiritual yearning among American Jews. The comments that I have received from Jewish and Christian clergy and laity of many denominations convinced me that we have to "explode" the categories of religious living, going beyond ritual and into the everyday and the mundane.

My emphasis in this book is how we can become God's partners in our work — in the seemingly mundane world of nine-to-five. In some ways, *Putting God on the Guest List* was easy: It was about *restoring* meaning to a moment where the meaning had been *forgotten. Being God's Partner* has been a bigger challenge: It is about *creating* meaning in a place where the meaning had rarely been thought possible.

Being God's Partner is about *re-framing* your experiences. It's about looking at what you do in your life in an entirely different way. I could not write about every occupation and career, so I have selected some which you can generalize from to your own particular circumstance. For example, when I write about doctors, I don't just mean people in the medical profession.

I am referring to the capacity that each of us has, whatever we do, to promote healing through the way we relate to others with whom we work and who are the beneficiaries of our work.

At the end of each section, I present some questions designed to help you take the concepts into your life. Answer them or think about them at the end of the chapter. Or go back and do this after you've finished the entire book. The most important thing is to do it so this book will not just be an intellectual experience, but a spiritual exercise that will help you turn thought into deed.

Introduction *by Norman Lear*

Walter Lippman once spoke of the church, the family, education and civil authority as "that old ancestral order" which was largely responsible for purveying values to the society. As these institutions and their impact on the culture waned, American business filled the vacuum. This continued to such an extent that business became the fountainhead of values in our society.

The mythologist Joseph Campbell had an arresting metaphor to describe the shift from the "old ancestral order" to today's order of commerce and finance. When one approached a city in medieval times, the tallest structure that could be seen on the skyline was the church and its steeple. As the power and influence of the church gave way to kings and rulers, the castle dominated the skyline. Today, as one approaches the city, the most commanding structures are the skyscrapers, the cathedrals of modern business.

To Campbell's marvelous metaphor, I add the phenomenon

of television. This is such an effective, all-pervasive medium that it has transferred the values of corporate America to American society. By piping the messages of American business — pitches for cars, shampoo and assorted and sundry widgets — into virtually every American home, it has made the term "consumer" a substitute for the term "citizen."

What is notable about this contemporary fountainhead of values is not simply the message that can be reduced to the five-word phrase: "We are what we consume." It is the overweening commitment of American business, not to qualitative values, but to quantitative values. We define ourselves, our values and our aspirations by SAT scores, Nielsen ratings, box office grosses, cost-benefit analysis, quarterly profits, bottom lines, and polls, polls, polls. All of these exert an iron grip on our sense of the possible, and on our very identities. As a numbers-oriented culture, we place our faith on what we can graph, chart or count, and we are suspicious of the unquantifiable, the intuitive, the mysterious.

A culture that becomes a stranger to its own inner human needs — needs which are unquantifiable, intuitive, mysterious — has lost touch with the best of its humanity; with that portion of itself that impels us to create art and literature and to study ethics, philosophy and history; with the part of our being that gives rise to our sense of awe and wonder; with our innate longing for a higher order of meaning. This is the spiritual life of our species, that aspect of ourselves that we have long recognized sets us apart from other creatures.

I cannot recall American culture being so estranged from

this essential part of itself. It is apparent in the loss of faith in leaders and institutions and in the cynicism, selfishness, erosion of civility and hunger for connectedness that are so commonplace in our nation. It is almost palpable in our quest as consumers for the latest gadgets or the fastest cars that virtually negate the inner life. And to return for a moment to the world of numbers, it is also sadly, abjectly quantifiable: Seventy-two percent of young adults now consider career success their most important goal in life. They apparently believe that there is nothing between winning and losing.

Most Americans are aware that we, as a nation, are not enjoying our material success. To scan today's cultural landscape is to see a burgeoning underclass, a growing army of homeless people, and an increasingly frustrated, alienated, economically hard-pressed middle class. We see drugs, crime, violence, racism, hate crimes, mindless massacres and children killing children. We find deteriorating cities and crumbling infrastructures.

What we draw from this litany of ills may vary. But lift the veil of partisan postures, and I suspect that most of us will admit that our problems lie beyond the reach of politics alone.

Everything in me says that the world would be an exquisite place if everyone responded to life with the understanding that comes when one's common sense derives as much from the soul as the mind. Ever since I smoked my first good cigar in my early 20's, I have felt that if there was no other reason to believe in God, it would have to be Havana leaf. I've also had the same sentiments while biting into a ripe peach, a just-ready piece of Crenshaw melon or a great ear of corn. I've sensed God's presence sitting in the back of a dark theater when a comedy was playing, watching an audience of 600 strangers coming forward, rising in their seats and then falling back, as people do when they are laughing from the belly. And I've experienced God's presence in the faces of my wife, my children, my grandson — and every time throughout my working life when I've gone to bed with a problem and awakened in the morning with the solution.

There was a time when I couldn't say this because I didn't feel qualified in this arena. Religion in our popular culture has a language — and I didn't have it. Then, a noted theologian who is a good friend suggested that I read William James' *The Varieties of Religious Experience* and there I was: Between the lines, between the experiences.

Many of us, perhaps the majority, are in a similar position. And we must not allow this territory to be preempted by "experts" who claim that their distinctive theology, tradition, or sizable membership gives them a special stamp of superiority and a greater right to be heard. It is precisely this spiritual arrogance and intolerance that has stifled a frank, comprehensive discussion of what it means to have a living faith in this troubled time. The sectarian rivalry and bickering about moral superiority and spiritual infallibility has already assumed a greater importance than the religious experience itself.

In 1988, Jeff Greenfield of ABC News said that reporters would have known that the social and political revolution known as "the civil rights movement" was about to explode if they had been more aware about what was going on in the basements of black churches in the 1950's. They would have been better prepared for the emergence of such people as Rosa Parks, Martin Luther King, Jr., Fanny Lou Hamer and other activists.

A phenomenon of equal significance is building now. It is a buzzing, disconnected eruption of spiritual reaction to our times; it is operating without the sanction of the popular culture or organized religion; and it can be used to shatter the walls erected by secularists and, even, religionists that prevent us from even talking about it.

This book by Rabbi Salkin is part of that phenomenon. Too often, we divorce our "work life" from our "real life," from our innermost beliefs and convictions. But "work" can be as much a part of our life — and as much a vehicle for spiritual growth and personal understanding — as going to synagogue or church on Saturday or Sunday or taking a walk in the woods or reading quietly to our kids at bedtime. In fact, work may be among the most potent vehicles for fulfilling our spiritual life because, for many of us, it presents the best opportunities to meld community and social and economic productivity with personal belief and individual talent. To let such an opportunity slip through our fingers is to discard a precious gift.

The challenge of our time is to live up to one of our nation's founding credos: "E Pluribus Unum," "Out of many, one." That feeling of unity without uniformity most certainly will not emerge from politics or economics as we know them today. It can only emerge from honoring that capacity that is unique to our species: The capacity for awe, wonder, mystery, art, music, love, compassion; by honoring the very search — and the very need — for higher meaning.

We all need to understand not just the creeds and the faith rivalries that divide us, but the rich capacity for religious experience that unites us; to nurture the desire we all possess for some invisible means of support — and to deliver to one another the way the universe delivers to us. And to remember, especially in our culture that puts such emphasis and faith on numbers, that, indeed, there is one number that truly has meaning and power and the ability to speak to each of us: The number one — or in Hebrew, "Echad," which, in Judaism, is another term for God, the Oneness within us and around us, and before which all other numbers pale.

One

Smuggling Religion into Work

A man lamented to his rabbi:
"I'm frustrated that my work leaves me no time for study or prayer."
The rabbi replied: "Perhaps your work is more pleasing to God than study or prayer."
— *Hasidic tale*

While walking in a neighboring village late at night, a Hasidic rebbe met a man who was also walking alone. For a while, the two walked in silence. Finally, the rebbe turned to the man and asked, "So, who do you work for?"

"I work for the village," the man answered. "I'm the night watchman."

They walked in silence again. Finally, the night watchman asked the rebbe, "And who do *you* work for?"

The rebbe answered, "I'm not always sure. But this I will tell you. Name your present salary and I will double it. All you have to do is walk with me and ask me, from time to time, *'Who do you work for?'*"

Many people ask themselves the same question. They work very hard. They know their job titles. They know their job descriptions. They know who their boss is. But they want to know for *Whom* they really work.

We Americans work very hard. So hard, that we often put

work at the emotional and spiritual center of our lives. Professionals work an average of 52 hours a week; college-educated workers in their 20s and 30s work even more. The amount of time that we spend at work has been steadily rising over the past 60 years. A 1933 law limited the work week to 30 hours. In 1938, the Fair Labor Standards Act provided for a work week of 40 hours. In 1948, 13 percent of Americans with full-time jobs worked more than 49 hours a week. By 1989, the Bureau of Labor Statistics estimated that of 88 million Americans with full-time jobs, 24 percent worked more than 49 hours a week. As Juliet B. Schor estimated in *The Overworked American: The Unexpected Decline of Leisure*, Americans report that, after their jobs and household duties are done, they have only 16 hours a week for leisure. To put Americans' working habits into perspective, manufacturing employees in the United States work 320 more hours — *the equivalent of two months* more — than their counterparts in Germany and France.

We Seek Meaning in Our Fragmented Lives

And yet, we suspect there is more to life than just working and accumulating goods and wealth. We yearn for something deeper that will make meaning of our fragile existences. From 9-to-5, we work hard. From 5-to-9, we are with our families or our hobbies or our friends or our various entertainments. And on Saturdays and Sundays, we (or, at least, some of us) are with our God, briefly and fleetingly. It's one of the reasons we lead fragmented lives — and one of the reasons that we wonder why all the disparate pieces of our selves somehow just don't fit together.

But, in reality, we rarely let those various compartments of our lives speak to each other or touch each other. We do our best to keep religion insulated from the rest of our life and the rest of the week. Attending to God and ethics and morals for a few hours on a weekend evening or morning is about as much time — and about as much credence — as many of us are willing to give to religion. Other than that, we rope religion off from what we "really" do, either afraid that it might "contaminate" our lives or convinced that it has little bearing upon it. As a result, our lives are often empty, unsatisfying, frustrating. We are like the central character in Saul Bellow's *Henderson the Rain King* who screams, "I want I want I want." He cannot name what he wants. Neither can most of us. But the longing is there.

Religious Answers Can Help Make Our Lives Whole

The contemporary quest for meaning was reflected by the questions pollster Daniel Yankelovich heard from young adults in a recent survey. In the 1950s and 1960s, the average American was asking questions such as: "Will I be able to make a good living?" "Will I be successful?" "Will I raise happy, healthy, successful children?" By the 1970s, Americans had turned more introspective. They asked: "How can I find self-fulfillment?" "What does personal success really mean?" "What kind of commitments should I be making?" "What is worth sacrificing for?" "How can I grow?"

These are religious questions because every question about ultimate meaning is a religious question. "Can work be spiritually uplifting?" "Can we stop viewing our work as drudgery, as something that just gets us through the week?" "Can we glean some Godly value from how we earn a dollar and how we define ourselves as workers?" To help satisfy this spiritual yearning, a few companies in the United States now follow the model of the armed forces and police and fire departments: They provide chaplains to offer non-denominational spiritual counseling to workers. These firms understand that we are whole people, incapable of shelving our spirits during our work hours.

To paraphrase the Jewish theologian Franz Rosenzweig, "Religion has to be smuggled into life." It also has to be smuggled into our work. I believe that modern Jews need to hear the voice of religion in their work. This will not only immeasurably enrich our inner lives; it is also the next vista in the American Jew's spiritual search. While this book talks about the Jewish tradition, and talks particularly to Jews, I believe that hearing the Jewish answer to questions of ultimate meaning can also offer Christians a model for how they might embark upon their own spiritual journey through their everyday life and work.

Why? Because over the past half century, the Protestant work ethic has become a true interfaith venture. American Jews have one of the highest socioeconomic and professional profiles in the nation. But such status comes at a severe price.

As a congregational rabbi, I increasingly hear people asking the hard questions about their work lives and their careers. I hear about it in my study and in conversations with other clergy — Jewish and Christian. I come across it in stray conversations with other parents as we watch our kids play soccer or Little League. I meet many people who are spiritually burnt-out from their work. I meet many who are disillusioned with their professions. We're working harder, but spiritually and emotionally, we're getting less out of it. Look no further than the bestseller lists to see how deep the American spiritual hunger truly is — books about near-death experiences; books about virtue; the remarkable success of Thomas Moore's book *The Care of the Soul* or Stephen Carter's *The Culture of Disbelief.* One does not have to be a radical to note that there are some major glitches in the capitalist system we have created. We sense that we have become spiritually damaged by the pernicious cycle of working/wanting/having as ends in themselves. What happens to family life when a home becomes a motel to sleep in between business trips? What happens to stability when mobility is the price of advancement? What happens to meaning when much of life is a blur?

Let Religion into the "Real World"

Once upon a time, "religion" and "life" were seamless. Not only did we pray these words from Deuteronomy twice a day, but we *believed* them: "Hear O Israel, the Lord our God, the Lord is One. And you shall love the Lord your God with all your heart, with all your soul, and with all your might....Speak these words when you sit in your house and when you walk by the way."

Religion was not just about how you prayed. It was also about what you learned; what you wore; how you behaved sexually; what you ate; how you cared for your body; if, when, and how you waged war; what you did with articles you found; with whom you traded. As the Talmud states, "Whoever says that the words of Torah are one thing and that the affairs of the world are another thing is like one who has no God." Claiming that religion is one thing and that "the real world" is another is tantamount to atheism.

But somewhere along the way, we asked religion to be silent about what people did in their everyday lives. As religion became increasingly relegated to life's leisure moments, for many people it had less of an orienting influence in their lives than a hobby.

Because of that, work and faith now rarely speak to one another. As Thomas Wuthnow, a Princeton University sociologist of religion, has noted, contemporary religion says "nothing at all about the material life, except to voice an occasional jab at the worship of Mammon [materialism], adding hastily that there is nothing wrong with money as long as we do not love it too much."

When Wuthnow asked lay people if religious beliefs had influenced their career choices, a great majority emphatically answered in the negative. Most did not think of their work as a calling. When asked how religion influenced their work or how they thought about money, most said the two realms were completely discrete.

This split between religion and the material world is not new. For Jews, it started in the late 18th and the early 19th centuries and has continued well into our time. The French Revolution, the Enlightenment and Emancipation (the growth of secularism and the acceptance of Jews into Western society) pushed religion out of the public realm and into the private sphere. Modernity demanded that we keep multiple sets of file folders — one for religion, for work, for family, for "the real world." Yehudah Leib Gordon, a 19th century Jewish writer, put this bifurcation of "life" and religion another way: "Be a Jew in your home and an undifferentiated human being on the streets." This became the credo of liberal Judaism during the last century. Religion was not only private; it should also know when to keep its mouth shut.

During the massive Eastern European Jewish immigration to America between 1880 and 1920, most who arrived here were not the most religiously observant people. The truly observant heeded their rabbis' denunciations of America as a *trefe medina*, a ritually impure land. Most stayed in Europe — and their children died at the hands of the Nazis.

In my wildest imaginings, I suspect that if skin divers dove into New York harbor, they would dredge up an underwater mountain of *tefillin* (phylacteries used for prayer). As the boats carrying our great-grandfathers passed by the Statue of Liberty, they literally kissed their *tefillin* goodbye. Religious observance was for another land and another place. They had to earn a living in their new country. Yes, they wanted to retain a sense of *yiddishkeit* (feelings of folk Jewishness). But *yiddishkeit* did not necessarily produce spiritual depth. Questions about work and its role in the inner life were luxuries to a generation that wanted to "succeed" in America.

For many, God became a hobby. "Enlightened" German Jews did not choose to ask the hard questions about religion and everyday life. Religion was relegated to the synagogue, just as for many Christians it was relegated to the church. Newly arrived Eastern European immigrant Jews knew how to ask the hard questions about the purpose of life. Generations of living in an environment of Talmudic study and the give-and-take of the Jewish legal process had taught them that. But here in America, they willfully forgot the methodology. They thought they could not afford to ask the questions.

That is how the part of Judaism that speaks to the inner life lost its voice.

We Must Stop Feeling Desperate

While many contemporary Jews are ready to start integrating the religious voice into their daily lives, new thought and bold actions are needed to achieve this. Letting faith speak to us in our work will provide fulfillment instead of the "lives of quiet desperation" to which Henry David Thoreau referred. It will orient us toward meaningful work and help shatter our egocentricity since it will teach us to simultaneously serve others, transcend ourselves, and, hopefully, encounter the very

Presence of God.

Letting spirituality and faith speak to us in our work will teach us to move beyond ambition and success, to stop worshipping at the false altars of career and prestige. As part of that process, we will learn that the original meaning of "career" is "that which you carry." We will learn what meanings we, as Jews, carry into the world.

Letting spirituality and faith speak to us in our work will remind us of Judaism's precious gift to the world: The idea of *mitzvah,* of holy obligation. We will learn that the 9-to-5 world is as much the arena for *mitzvot* as is our discretionary time.

Letting spirituality and faith speak to us in our work will teach us to act on the basis of our better moral impulses and values. It will help us be more creative and socially responsible. It will also increase our enthusiasm for our work, especially when work becomes wearisome, and help us avoid burnout and stress.

Letting spirituality and faith speak to us — and hearing that voice in our workplaces — will extinguish the false distinction between the world of the spirit and the world of the market. The Jewish people do not have the right to put on their Jewish hats at their convenience. The necessary coherence between religion and life is why tradition dictates that the Torah scroll be carried into the congregation before it is read. The Torah must leave the relative safety of the *aron ha-kodesh* (the Holy Ark) so it can enter the world — and enter our lives.

Finally, letting religion speak to us in our work can help us integrate the many facets of our being and give them meaning. There needs to be a place within us where professional, parent, spouse, friend, child, sibling — *and Jew* — come together and speak as *one.* If God is One, and if we truly *know* that, then our lives become a conscious imitation of God as its disparate pieces meld together. That consciousness will open us to a real inner joy and satisfaction.

Is There a Jewish Spirituality of Work?

When the world was very young, there was a moment when life was as close to perfection as it has ever been — and as close to perfection as it will be until the Messiah comes. This was in the Garden of Eden, where God gave Adam a single task: "Till the garden and guard it."

The Garden was beautiful and luscious. Adam's experience in it was similar to that of a guest at a king's banquet. His task was holy because God had told him to do it; it spiritually satisfied him because he knew God wanted him to do it. The Garden of Eden was a collaborative effort between God and Adam. It is a metaphor for all life and for the entire world — and for the world of work.

Because Eve told Adam to eat from the Tree of Knowledge of Good and Evil, she was punished with the pain of childbirth. Adam's punishment was that his labors would be henceforth difficult. "Cursed be the ground because of you," God told him. "By toil shall you eat of it all the days of your life. Thorns and thistles shall it sprout for you. But your food shall be the grasses of the field. By the sweat of your brow shall you get bread to eat" (Genesis 3:19).

Adam's punishment was not necessarily *labor* since he had already worked in the Garden. His curse was that he would have to do sweaty, tiring, often frustrating toil to bring forth bread from a sometimes uncooperative earth. In essence, this is the Jewish spirituality of work. Work, which would no longer be easy, would be how humanity could make the world more holy and complete the work that God had started.

Many generations later, the curse of Eden was demonically fulfilled in Egypt. There, the Israelites endured difficult, demeaning work intended to break their bodies and their spirits. Paradoxically, the experience of slavery forged them into a nation. When they left Egypt, they traded coercion under Pharaoh for covenant with God.

In the wilderness, God sustained the Israelites with manna, the mysterious "bread from heaven." Manna stopped falling once they entered the land of Israel. They, not God, would now be responsible for their own sustenance. As the great moral philosopher Bachya wrote in Spain in the 11th century, "Man's [*sic*] livelihood requires his active participation. Apart from the period of the wandering in the wilderness, or other instances of miraculous intervention for limited periods, there is no manna from heaven. This active participation of man in the creation of his own wealth is a sign of man's spiritual greatness. In this respect, he is an imitator of God."

In ancient Israel, Jews were farmers, traders, bankers and merchants. Trade and crafts flourished in the few cities that existed. In Jerusalem, certain professions lived and worked in specific districts. The Bible even refers to the city's "valley of craftsmen" (I Chronicles 4:14) and "bakers' street" (Jeremiah 37:21).

Biblical law was concerned with workers' welfare and dignity. Prophets preached in the marketplace, not from a podium in the Temple in Jerusalem. They mercilessly denounced those employers who did not pay their workers on time. The prophet known as the Second Isaiah railed against his people's economic sins: "Why, when we fasted, did You not see? When we starved our bodies, did You pay no heed? Because on your fast day you see to your business and oppress all your laborers!" (Isaiah 58:3). Jeremiah castigated anyone "who builds his house with unfairness, and his upper chambers with injustice, who makes his fellow man work without pay and does not give him his wages" (Jeremiah 22:13). Amos denounced the economic sins of the upper-class, such as allowing financial gain to override justice and ignoring the plight of the poor (Amos 2:6 and 4:1).

Idleness was a social evil. As Proverbs states, "Whoever is slack in his work is brother to him that destroys" (Prov. 18:9). Those who needed a lesson in industriousness were told to observe the ways of the lowly ant (Prov. 6:6). Work was the route to personal happiness and fulfillment: "If you eat the fruit of the labor of your hands, you will be happy and prosperous" (Psalms 128:2).

The Balanced Life is Our Goal

In the first century of the Common Era, some Jewish sages tried to escape the difficulties of Roman rule by retreating into otherworldliness. Some sages even deprecated work, believing that the only true labor was the study of Torah and the work of the spirit. A tale in the Talmud echoed some early sages' philosophical wrestling about whether we live in the "real world" or in the world of the spirit: About 130 C.E. (the Common Era), several Jews were debating how the Romans had affected the land of Israel. "How noble are the works of this Roman nation!" one sage raved. "They laid out streets, they built bridges, they erected baths." But Rabbi Shimon bar Yochai said, "All that they made, they made to serve themselves. They laid out streets to settle harlots in them; baths, to pamper themselves; bridges, to levy tolls."

Word got back to the Roman authorities about what Shimon bar Yochai had said. When they issued a warrant for his arrest, the rabbi and his son escaped to a cave where a carob tree and a well were miraculously created for their sustenance. They studied and prayed there for 12 years.

Finally, the prophet Elijah told bar Yochai and his son that the decree against them had been annulled. They emerged from the cave and, seeing Jews plowing and sowing, the rabbi exclaimed, "These people forsake life eternal and engage in life temporal!" Whatever bar Yochai and his son cast their eyes upon was immediately incinerated. An angry God finally roared at them, "Have you come out to destroy My world?

Return to your cave!" (Talmud, *Shabbat* 33a).

Did only Roman persecution send bar Yochai and his son into hiding? No. He and his son had escaped to a cave (which symbolizes the *womb)* where they *regressed.* They did not labor for their food and had almost no material comforts to satisfy. They had, in effect, re-attached themselves to their umbilical cords and re-entered a world where their bodies were secondary to their spirits.

But there is more. Rabbi Shimon and his son could not tolerate the world. They were so fixated on the inner world of the spirit that they could not tolerate those who plowed and sowed in an effort to transform *this* world. God told them that castigating those who plant and sow was tantamount to destroying the world.

This lesson applies to all of us: Living a balanced life means leaving the womb of easy existence and entering into a partnership with God dedicated to sustaining the world, to making it productive, to reaping its benefits, to making it all it can be. It means leaving the womb of easy existence and leading lives of challenge and productivity.

This story is crucial to a balanced, realistic Jewish spirituality. It warns that the life of the spirit should not sequester the individual from the real world. Commenting on this tale in the Talmud, Rabbi Yishmael stressed that we should each study Torah, but that God's plan for the world requires us to also provide for his or her material needs. Each person, believed the Talmudic sages, was endowed with a *yetzer ha-tov,* a good, pure inclination, and a *yetzer ha-ra,* an evil, aggressive inclination. Yet, the *yetzer ha-ra* had some redeeming qualities: "Without the evil inclination, no one would father a child, build a house, or make a career." This aggressive, active, ambitious part of the human psyche could not be denied since it was essential to maintaining and propagating the world.

Combining Torah study with work eventually became accepted Jewish wisdom. Although Rabbi Yishmael came from a wealthy family, he taught that we should all be involved in practical everyday affairs and not retreat from life by becoming monastic. To him, "You shall choose life" (Deuteronomy 30:19) meant choosing a trade to make a living. But he also counselled, "One who wishes to acquire wisdom should study the way money works, for there is no greater area of Torah-study than this" (Talmud, *Baba Batra* 175b).

The greatest window into the rabbinic way of understanding work is through the rabbis' vocabulary. One word, *avodah*, came to mean not only "work," but also prayer, Torah study, and sacrifices in the ancient Temple in Jerusalem. What all these meanings had in common was their potential ability to lift each of us out of ourselves and to let us touch something deeper and higher in the world.

Maimonides, the great medieval sage, taught that we should equally divide our time among 1) studying Torah; 2) earning a livelihood; and 3) necessary physical activities, such as eating and sleeping. He never questioned that studying Torah took precedence over the other two.

The ancient rabbis elevated work to the level of a *mitzvah* (a holy obligation) since the Torah commands "six days you shall labor" before it demands that we rest on the Sabbath. They said that a father was obligated to teach his son a trade: "Whoever does not teach his son a trade has taught him robbery." These sages had "real" jobs: Hillel was a woodcutter; Shammai, a builder; Rabbi Joshua, a blacksmith; Rabbi Hanina, a shoemaker. They understood the scruffy, gritty, workaday world because they worked in it; they recognized its limits and their responsibility to it. When, for instance, some rabbis were discussing how the world had been created, they said, "Let us go ask Rabbi Joseph the Builder, for there is no one better versed in these matters."

They found the rabbi working on some scaffolding. "I cannot go down to answer," he said, "for I was hired by the day and my time belongs to my employer."

Rather than answering obscure questions about the origins of the cosmos, Rabbi Joseph knew that his job — *at that particular moment* — was to be engaged in the seemingly mundane world of work. Rather than engage in games of intellectual speculation, as a builder he could imitate and complete, in his limited way, God's work of creation.

The way of Shimon bar Yochai — the way of the cave and of withdrawal from the material world — never became the way of Judaism. *Parnassah*, or material benefit that is honestly gained and never placed at the center of one's being, is part of the Jewish people's spiritual vocabulary. To them, money and possessions were never a curse, as they were considered by more mystical religions in the ancient Near East. Instead, Judaism taught that money, possessions and work were essentially *neutral*, yet eminently powerful in their ability to transform or destroy. All three could be used to improve the world. Even on Yom Kippur, the holiest day of the year, Jews reflect upon the material world. And even as God opens the Book of Judgement, the Holy One also opens the *sefer parnassah*, a book of economic and material welfare, and Jews pray to be inscribed in it as well.

Our Work Can Make Us Immortal

A simple perusal of Jewish holy texts like the Talmud or the *Shulchan Aruch* reveals that, over the centuries, Jewish scholars spent more time interpreting the meaning of *non-work* (e.g., *Shabbat*) than the meaning of work itself. When they *did* look at the world of work, most of their concern centered on ethical issues connected with such professions as medicine, or on the intricacies of labor law. As Marshall J. Breger, a senior fellow at the Heritage Foundation in Washington, D.C., has suggested, traditional Jews never invested significant meaning in their jobs. Such meaning came from activities completely outside of work: Religious study, charity, and family life. The relevant question about a job was whether it provided enough to support one's family and afforded one the time to study. Work was a means, not an end. It was a *part* of the journey, not the entire journey. One was not, therefore, defined by one's job.

Judaism's stance toward work and spirituality is also suggested by its teachings regarding immortality. During the Middle Ages, it was common to chisel on tombstones insignias of the professions of the deceased. When people were buried, the casket was often constructed from the wooden table upon which the deceased had worked: Even after death, our work was part of who we were, and what we carried into eternity.

Since work is what we leave behind in this world, it could be a way to achieve personal immortality. When we study Maimonides, his words are his immortality. When we read Shakespeare or see one of his plays performed, we glimpse his place in mortality. Hearing Mozart's music means that he has, in one sense, conquered death.

So, too, does the designer of the classic Mustang, the doctor who saves lives, the lawyer who helps a defendant, a secretary who creates an efficient filing system, an architect who designs and builds a building: All are immortal. Their work survives them. Every teacher's *Kaddish* is his or her students. As a friend said, "Every time I recommend a book to my child to read, and that book had been recommended to *me* by Mrs. Cohen, my fourth grade teacher, that's Mrs. Cohen's immortality."

The late philosopher Hannah Arendt knew the eternal value of our labors. "Work and its product, the human artifact," she wrote, "bestow a measure of permanence and durability upon the futility of mortal life and the fleeting character of human time."

"We Have Come to Build And to Be Re-built"

But the real revolution in how Jews would come to think of

work would come with the single biggest revolution in modern Jewish thinking and endeavor: Zionism.

In the late 19th century, Zionism began to revolutionize Judaism's attitude toward the world. For centuries, most Jews had been secluded in the ghettos of Europe and the *mellahs* (restricted communities) of the Moslem world. The early Zionists not only wanted to build a land. They wanted to bring Jews from the reclusiveness of the ghetto into engagement with the larger world. Zionism became a metaphoric rejection of Jewish passivity.

Nothing was more symbolic of this new Jewish activism than physical work, and no work more crucial to early Zionism than farming in Eretz Yisrael. This would connect Jews to the land, the soil, and the rough realities of life. Zionist folk songs echoed the Socialist hymns of Europe and extolled the virtue of labor: "The pioneer exists for the sake of labor, and labor exists for the sake of the pioneer"; "We have come to the Land to build it and to be built up by it."

Aharon David Gordon (1856–1922), a Zionist pioneer and thinker, clearly saw the link between *avodah* (worship) and *avodah* (labor). He believed that God could be approached through physical labor. Influenced by Leo Tolstoy, the Russian mystic and writer, Gordon celebrated agricultural work as a supreme act of personal, national, and cosmic redemption. He believed that, by integrating the workers with the "organic rhythms" of nature and the universe, toiling on the land let them experience the unity and purpose of the cosmos. For Gordon, this was the core religious experience.

And, in fact, it may become true for our generation as well. To work in the world can be our way of stating that we have a hand in the orderly maintenance of the cosmos.

Making It Real in Your Life

- *For whom do you work?*
- *How does your work help you articulate ideals and values that you find holy?*
- *Does your religious faith influence your work?*
  Did it influence your choice of career?
- *Have you made compromises between your spiritual life and your work life? How can you change what you are doing?*
- *Does your work give you the opportunity to perform* mitzvot*?*
- *Do you believe that your work can help you find a piece of immortality?*
- *What's the first step you can take to bring balance to your life?*

Two

What Is Spirituality, Anyway?

"The ineffable Name of God: We have forgotten how to pronounce it. We have almost forgotten how to spell it. We may totally forget how to recognize it."
— *Abraham Joshua Heschel*

For many people, "work" and "spirituality" negate and contradict each other; they are polar opposites that come from two entirely different universes.

Such individuals may be well-versed in the concept of "work": They do it almost every day. But they do not properly understand the concept of "spirituality." To them, "work" is wholly practical, rooted in the necessities of this world and geared toward providing for self and family. "Spirituality," on the other hand, is otherworldly, ethereal and has little bearing on what seems to be one of the most mundane, demanding and unavoidable aspects of our lives: Our jobs and our professions.

For them, the concept of spirituality has to be reconstructed, almost from the ground up. These doubters have to reorient themselves to spirituality's surprising practicality, to its broad applications to every facet of our lives, and to the surprising symmetry it has with work.

But this is hard for many of us to believe. That difficulty arises because of our preconceived notions about the nature of spirituality, work, and "the real world."

As a rabbi, I have heard many misconceptions from lay people about spirituality. Below are some of the most frequently voiced opinions about spirituality — and how I respond to them.

Work is about being active. Isn't spirituality basically a passive stance towards the world?

Sometimes, but *only* sometimes.

By "passive" spirituality, I mean those moments when God's light and grace seem to flow almost on their own volition into our lives. Some of this is admittedly "foxhole" theology: A faith that comes upon you in the midst of a crisis or an emergency: "I was almost run over by a car, but God saved me" or "I was sure my baby would die of pneumonia, but something stronger than medicine saved her."

Such a moment of faith is very Jewish. It is the faith of Moses, who, upon asking God, "Let me see your glory [*kavod*]!" hears God responding, "I will let all my goodness pass before you." *Kavod* is usually translated as "divine glory," but a better translation is "a moment of divine, ineffable wonder."

This is also the faith of the Psalmist, who often speaks of God's miraculous redeeming presence. On a communal level, it is the events that we commemorate on a holiday such as

Passover (and to a lesser extent on Purim) when the entire Jewish people felt God's power in history.

But spirituality is more than feeling that you have been temporarily lifted from the mundane world. Spirituality is *active* as well as *passive.* This means that we search for and intentionally *create* moments and possibilities in which our eyes open to a reality that is beyond us, yet very much part of us.

No wonder many of us have trouble relating spirituality to work. If we think that work is active, and that spirituality is passive, how can work be spiritual? But *if* we realize that we can be active agents of God in the world, then we can fulfill some of our Jewish duties even while we're on the job.

I've had spiritual experiences and feelings, but I only know about them after they've happened. You can't really plan for this to happen — certainly not in your work.

This is 20-20 hindsight spirituality. *Something* may have connected us to a higher and deeper reality, but the experience came, it went, and now it's gone. The next time it comes will be truly wonderful, but one can't really make it happen.

Yet, it is possible to create a mindset, an attitude, a posture that will help us experience the world anew — and not merely *ruminate* upon a past experience that was uplifting. It is also possible to *plan* to experience something, such as work, spiritually.

One thing we can do is to *re-frame* our experiences. This means that we choose to interpret our experiences so that we see them as pathways to God. I believe that Judaism wants it no other way. Hasidic masters inserted meditations (*kavannot*) throughout the texts of their prayer books. These were intended to focus worshippers' minds and souls on the essence of the immediate spiritual task. Everything we do is subject to contemporary *kavannot* that can help us focus on the higher implications of our actions.

Such focusing, of course, means being radically open to such experiences and having a vivid, creative imagination. Abraham H. Maslow, the pioneering humanistic psychologist, called mystical, illuminating, transcendent moments "peak experiences." Spirituality brings peak experiences to everyday life; it is the ability — and the desire — to find those junctures where our reality and God's reality intersect; it is learning how to feel God in every part and every moment of our life.

How can we talk about God being in our work if spirituality happens in the "other" world, not in this world?

"Spirituality" is not the opposite of "worldliness." We should not let our heads soar into the clouds if our feet are not anchored on the ground. To do so is to lose any sense of mundane reality — a reality that we need to survive in this world. We do not need to flee to other worlds to feel the presence of God: Holiness exists in *this* world and in the rhythms of daily existence.

Hasidism teaches the doctrine of *avodah be-gashmiyut,* of worshipping God through such physical acts as eating, drinking, sex, and even through the way we conduct business. Consciousness about such seemingly mundane acts lets us redeem the sparks of holiness that are present in the world; it prevents us from succumbing to the dangers of an overwrought spirituality that distances us from the realities of existence.

Perhaps the most potent lesson of Jewish spirituality is that redemption resides in *this* world. As the late Jewish theologian Abraham Joshua Heschel wrote, "God will return to us when we shall be willing to let Him in — into our lands and our factories, into our Congress and clubs, into our courts and investigating committees, into our homes and theaters." Heschel found spirituality in political action. Walking alongside Martin Luther King, Jr. in Selma, Alabama, he felt, for example, that "my feet were praying." Deuteronomy 30:12 also tries to keep our spiritual feet on the ground: "It [the Torah and God's teachings] is not in the heavens." *It* is in every moment of our lives, in our every action, in our work.

Isn't spirituality about emotion? And isn't work about the rational mind?

Some people define spirituality as "religion *plus* emotion." *Religion* in one's work is hard enough. But *emotion*? Many people believe that work can't be about emotion. As a doctor told me, "You'll lose your mind if you do nothing but *feel* all the time at work. Sometimes work just *has* to be routine." Moreover, in the compartmentalized way that we sometimes view the world, *work* is the rational arena and *religion* is the place where emotions take over. Mixing the two would be a categorical violation of the highest order.

Some people might argue that totally severing our emotions from our work would make us even more effective in our careers. But would it be worth it?

I don't think so. Such a severing of emotions from the work world would only further contribute to the mind/body split so common today. Jewish spirituality asks us to strive to be like God, to be *echad*, "one," just as God is One. By attempting to experience God in our work, we affirm that no sector of everyday experience is aloof from the divine.

I could find spirituality in "the real world," but it's a little scary.

As a doctor once told me, "You can find spirituality in your work. I do all the time. But a lot of people fear being *overwhelmed* by spirituality, and they automatically detach themselves from the potential spiritual experience in their work. Let's face it: Your ability to function credibly at work means leaving spirituality behind. You must set limits for yourself, or that spirituality will truly devour you."

Almost from its beginnings, Judaism acknowledged this fear of being spiritually overwhelmed. When Moses encountered God's presence in the burning bush, he "hid his face because he was afraid to look at God" (Ex. 3:6). Elsewhere, God told Moses: "No one can see My face and live" (Ex. 33:20). To be in God's presence was frightening. It still is frightening. We cower at the possibility at the same time that we seek it.

But can we *increase* such moments of closeness? And can they occur not only before bushes that burn, but also in the office?

We Can Re-build Meaning in Our Lives

Our ultimate mission is to become what Judaism calls *hamavdil beyn kodesh la-chol*: To make a difference between that which is already holy and that which, with a little effort, can become holy.

Some of the best, most powerful religious stories are paradoxical tales of people finding non-religious ways to express their faith. The Jewish theologian Martin Buber told of the little boy who brought his flute to play in the synagogue to show his devotion to God. It was the only thing that he knew how to do well. Some people can only work and make money. It is not the worst thing in the world to offer to God. Work, indeed, can be a very worthy offering to God.

After the Romans destroyed Jerusalem in 70 C.E., the sages of the beleaguered Jewish people fled to Yavneh, a small town in western Israel. There, they had a saying: "I am God's creature, and my fellow is God's creature. My work is in the city, and his [*sic*] work is in the country. I rise early for my work, and he rises early for his work. Just as he does not presume to do my work, so I do not presume to do his work. Will you say I do much and he does little?...One may do much or one may do little, it is all one, provided he directs his heart to heaven."

The ancient sages sought a place in which to re-create

Judaism and re-build meaning in their lives. But they also knew that *all work* — not just theirs — can be a source of holiness and that everyone has a task in God's divine plan.

Today's Jews are also living after a great destruction: The Holocaust. But the modern world knows of another destruction, one less bloody but no less traumatic: The destruction of meaning and value. Today, meaning itself must be reconstructed by finding spirituality in everyday experiences.

"Where is God?" asks a Hasidic teaching. "Wherever you let God in," comes the answer.

God wants to be allowed into our lives. Not only that, but God *needs* to enter the many hours and the many thoughts and the many worries that we devote to our work. Our careers consume much of our strength and our time and our creativity, but they must never consume us. If that occurs, we are dead to ourselves, to our colleagues at work, to our family at home.

One way to wake up to ourselves, to be truly alive, is to ask ourselves, as the Hasidic rebbe had the night watchman ask him, "Who do you work for?"

When the answer is clear, we will still work — for that is our purpose in life. But we will do it with a pure heart and with a more playful (and a more prayerful) soul.

Making It Real in Your Life

- ***When have you felt spirituality in the "passive" mode?***
- ***When have you felt spirituality in the "active" mode?***
- ***Is it possible to plan spiritual experiences?***
- ***Have you had any spiritual experiences in the everyday world? Under what circumstances?***
- ***How can you turn your work into an arena for spiritual experiences?***

Three

Imitating God

“Abraham and Sarah ‘created souls in Haran’ (Gen. 12:5). Isn’t that God’s job? By enlarging and uplifting the lives of those about them, they actually became their creators. In this way, they imitated God.”
— *Midrash*

In one of the final scenes in the film *Manhattan*, Ike, the Woody Allen character, challenges his friend Yale to be more self-critical about the ethics of his personal life.

Yale resists the challenge. “You are so self-righteous!” he screams. “We’re just people. We’re just human beings. You think you’re God!”

Ike shrugs his shoulders and says, “I gotta model myself after someone.”

As lofty, impossible and arrogant as it may sound, that is the beginning of the Jew’s spiritual mission: Imitating God.

Imitating God may seem strange to those who believe that God is distant, mysterious, and can be approached only with fear and trembling. Jewish lore teaches that Abraham, the first Jew, peered into the infinitude of the stars, and there discovered that transcendent side of God. When Abraham encountered God in the cosmos, he understood that there was a Presence behind all that he saw with his eyes and knew with his mind. Many of us believe in that distant God.

But those of us not satisfied with a distant God want a different kind of divinity, a God of intimacy. Some seek that aspect of God by meditating or engaging in other disciplines to become one with Oneness. But most Jews have known that the way to get close to God is to try to become *like* God. In this way, we transcend our own being and become more human by becoming more Godlike. As philosopher Erich Fromm said, "Man is not God, nor could he become God. He can become *like* God." Being like God is the twin of the notion that we are made in God's image. God is holy. "You shall be holy, for I the Eternal am holy" (Lev. 19:1).

Imitating God is common to both Jewish and Christian theological vocabularies. When Christianity speaks of the imitation of God (*imitatio dei*), it means imitating *Christ* because he is God incarnate. Christians emulate Jesus's thoughts, desires, intentions, virtues. They are also inspired by the saints because such persons were particularly expert at Christ-imitation and, therefore, at God-imitation.

Jews imitate God by directly imitating *God.* More than we realize, God's actions inspire Jewish faith and life. A good example of this is in the realm of ritual. When Jews light Shabbat candles at sundown on Friday, for instance, they become *domeh la'Kadosh Baruch Hu,* "akin to the Holy One," Who, during Creation, made the sun and the moon, which the two candles represent. Likewise, the act of removing the Torah scroll from the Ark and reading it is an imitation of God, Who revealed

Torah at Sinai.

Judaism believes that for theology to really "work," it has to be more than just abstract God-talk. Because of that, Jews think more about what they are supposed to *do* than about what God is *like*. When Jews come up with *adjectives* about God, they are really trying to discern what *their* lives should be.

In Exodus 34, Moses asked to see God's face. God refused this request since "no one can see Me and live." Instead, God told Moses about the divine essence: "Compassionate and gracious, slow to anger, abounding in kindness and faithfulness, extending kindness to the thousandth generation, forgiving iniquity, transgression, and sin..." (Ex. 34:6).

The early sages of the Midrash — the great teachers who created Judaism — took those attributes and said something that must have been radical: "You, O finite person — you can be like God." As the Midrash says: "Just as God is gracious and compassionate, you must be gracious and compassionate. Just as God is beneficent, you must be beneficent. Just as God is loving, you must be loving" (Midrash, *Sifre Deut.* 49). What God *is* becomes what we *do*. To discover our role in the world, we mimic God's role in human history: "God shows no favor, nor takes no bribe, but upholds the cause of widows and orphans, and befriends the stranger, providing him with food and clothing. You, too, must befriend the stranger, for you were strangers in the land of Egypt" (Deut. 10:17-19).

But the most basic understanding of what it means to imitate God is from the Talmud, in which Rabbi Hama, son of

Rabbi Hanina, asked what the Bible meant by stating, "You shall walk behind Adonai your God." Could a person truly walk behind God, Whom the Torah says is a "devouring fire"? Yes, all this is true. But to walk behind God means that we should imitate the ways of the Holy One.

"Just as God clothed Adam and Eve when they were naked," said Rabbi Hama, "*we* must supply clothes for the naked poor. Just as God visited Abraham when he was healing from his circumcision, *we* should visit the sick. Just as God buried Moses, *we* must bury the dead. Just as God comforted Isaac after the death of his mother Sarah, *we* should comfort mourners" (Talmud, *Sotah* 14a).

Think of God-imitation not only as an idea implicit in sacred texts, or as a lofty idea that seems too pompous and heavy-handed for every day life. Think of it not only as good works, or as charity, or as *noblesse oblige.* Instead, think of God-imitation as part of your professional code and your job description, as part of your moral resume, as part of how you do whatever you do. As audacious as it must sound, you can imitate God in your work.

By doing this, we can transform our work — or at the very least, how we *think* about our work — into something higher and deeper and more satisfying, both to us and to others. The idea of God-imitation is one that Jews and Christians share, and that unites sincere people of faith in their quest to find religious meaning and supernal significance in what they do.

Consider the following occupations and careers as models that you can follow to help connect your work to the holy.

Clothing the World

God's clothing of Adam and Eve was the first *mitzvah* in history, and the first act of *hesed*, "lovingkindness," mentioned in the Torah. Thus, every act of making, providing and selling clothing is an imitation of God.

I have a lot of friends in the garment business. I can't believe how stressed they are. When I recently asked a friend in the textile business whether he felt anything spiritual in his work, he looked at me as if I was slightly crazy. He knows about spirituality: He attends synagogue services every week and studies Torah on a regular basis.

"I really don't see anything terribly spiritual in what I do," he said. "This is a tough business. Sure, some people get involved in ethical issues. You remember that big thing about not using overseas labor, especially child labor? You think that was about oppression in the Third World? Of course not! Because prisoners in *this* country perform the same kind of oppressive labor. No, the real issue is competition from overseas workers. Foreign workers making clothing at low wages is unfair to American workers. It's very hard to find something spiritual in what I do."

The roots of the garment industry go back to Europe, but the masses of working-class Eastern European Jewish immigrants who came to this country helped it flourish here. In America, it became an almost totally Jewish industry. Of all the fields Jews entered in the United States, the garment industry seems almost *quintessentially* Jewish for it demonstrated Jews' ability to adapt and to create an industry virtually out of nothing.

I don't mean that the garment business was only *sociologically* Jewish. I mean that it is *spiritually* Jewish, as well. This is how that spirituality might manifest itself.

Those in the garment trades might look at their work as being *spiritually noble*, as a vehicle to the Jewish blessing that is traditionally said upon putting on new clothing: "Blessed are You, Eternal our God, Who clothes the naked." There is something miraculous in our everyday world: "I didn't have to have these clothes. Some people, perhaps *many* people, don't. Come to think of it, merely to be clothed and warm is a blessing. Thank you."

It is ennobling to see one's work as a *mitzvah* as well as a business. By "ennobling," I mean that which makes us feel that our lives are more important than we could ever know otherwise — that we are children of a Divine Ruler Who cares for us and has a mission for us to fulfill. Suddenly, life becomes richer and more significant. We may even behave differently.

For example, those in the bridal business can interpret their work as fulfilling the *mitzvah* of *hachnasat kallah,* helping the bride and groom celebrate a sacred moment in their lives, being part of the process that honors love, sanctifies relationship, builds a home — and might bring us another generation.

The Mishnah tells us that helping a couple celebrate their wedding is one of the deeds that bring people into the World to Come. With this in mind, perhaps, some people in the bridal business donate slightly out-of-fashion wedding apparel to brides with limited economic resources. For such brides must also celebrate their entry to matrimony.

It is ennobling to let even the little things in our work speak volumes about the human spirit and affect how we treat others. A few years ago, I officiated at the funeral of a woman who had been a clerk in a lingerie store. Her fellow workers eulogized her by remembering that when recovering mastectomy patients came into the shop to purchase brassieres, she treated them with utter compassion, delicacy and dignity. The Talmud tells us that "as God is compassionate, you, too, should be compassionate." Compassion is not always in the grand gesture. Sometimes it is in the little things. In God's economy of the human spirit, nothing is ever wasted. Her colleagues' tender stories about this simple woman are part of the draft of the American Talmud that someday will surely be written.

It is ennobling to be an integral link in the eternal chain of creativity itself. Ben Zoma, a first-century Jewish sage, said: "How many labors did Adam have to engage in before he obtained a garment to wear! He sheared the sheep, washed the wool, combed it, spun it, wove it, dyed the cloth, and sewed it. Only then did he have a garment to wear. But I get up and find all these things done for me" (Talmud, *Berachot* 58a). People who produce garments are part of a chain of creation that goes back to God. He or she imitates God by clothing the naked. He or she is also a creator.

The original Hasidim often told stories about people in various trades because they considered such tradespeople to be metaphors for spirituality. They especially thought garment makers evoked something higher and deeper than what was seen on the surface.

In fact, the Baal Shem Tov, the founder of Hasidism, once met a hosiery maker at synagogue and fruitlessly tried to bargain with him about the cost of his wares.

"How do you spend your days?" eventually asked the Baal Shem Tov.

"I ply my trade," said the man. "I work until I have 40 or 50 pairs of hose. Then I put them into a mold with hot water and press them until they are as they should be."

"And how do you sell them?" asked the Baal Shem Tov.

"The merchants come to me to buy. They also bring me good wool....Before I pray in the morning, I make hose. And while I work, I recite psalms which I know by heart."

When the hosemaker left, the Baal Shem Tov said to his disciples, "Today, you have seen the cornerstone which will uphold the Temple until the Messiah comes."

The hosemaker had integrated his work and his spirituality. He would not lower his price because he refused to bargain over the true value of his work. To him, making and selling were essential to his relationship with God. He worked while he prayed — or perhaps he prayed while he worked. For that reason, he was a holy person, a cornerstone of society and a model of piety.

Comforting the Bereaved

The first *mitzvah* in the Torah was clothing the naked. The last *mitzvah* is burying the dead. The funeral director can therefore imitate God, too. Anyone who comforts mourners, counsels and consoles the bereaved, helps people in their transitions from light to darkness and back also emulates God, Who comforted Isaac after the death of Abraham and Who buried Moses on Mount Nebo. That is why the Aramaic term for the traditional Jewish burial society is *hevra kaddisha*, "the holy fellowship." To bury the dead and to console the living is one of the holiest acts that anyone can perform.

Few professions carry as much negative baggage as the funeral business. It has been a source of scandal, embarrassment, skittishness, and even humor.

None of these accord with my experience. On the contrary, I have always admired the funeral directors with whom I've worked while in the rabbinate. They are sensitive, compassionate, ethically delicate, and, in their own right, leaders in the Jewish community.

Burying the dead has a curious name in Judaism: *Hesed ve-emet*, love and truth. Someone who helps people in their final journey also helps us encounter the great *truth* of the universe, hopefully with *hesed*, love and compassion. As a nurse recently told me, "Preparing bodies for burial is a true spiritual experience. I'll never get anything back for doing it. I am doing something for the deceased that can never be repaid. It is truly an unbegrudging kindness."

Some would say that it hardly matters how the dead are treated. But it *does*. It matters to *us*, the living. One of the hallmarks of Judaism is that it matters to God as well.

While recently driving to a funeral, I asked a young man who had just become a Jewish funeral director, "How did you get into this line of work?"

"Since I was always interested in the counseling end of the experience of death," he said, "in college I majored in thanatology [the study of death]. I finally decided to become a funeral director. When I got my program of courses, I saw classes in chemistry, biology and anatomy. I told my advisor, 'There seems to be some mistake, sir. My schedule shows me with all these science classes. I want to be a funeral director. What do these subjects have to do with it?'

"'Well,'" he said, 'you'll be dealing with cadavers, and those courses will be very important to you.'

"'Cadavers?' I asked in some panic. 'There seems to be some mistake. I want to be a funeral director: To counsel people, help them get over their losses, help them cope. What does that have to do with cadavers?'

"My advisor smiled slowly at me. 'It has *everything* to do with cadavers,' he said. 'That's the business. First, you deal with death. *Then* you deal with the survivors.'"

"What's spiritual about my work?" another funeral director asked.

"We try to bring families together. You'd be amazed how many families don't want to be in the same building as other members of the family. People sometimes take out their anger and their hurt at God and the world on the funeral director."

"As I prepare clients for a funeral, I always emphasize respect and dignity for the dead. I try to steer them towards how

Judaism views death, to teach about *keriah* [the traditional cutting of the cloth as a sign of mourning] and covering the grave. When people participate in such rituals, it helps them get in touch with their own spirituality and makes them less angry at God and more at peace with themselves.

"I am moved when clients tell me stories about their loved ones who were exceptional people. Sometimes, my job is to help people remember what should be remembered, to hold onto what should be held onto. For instance, even though it is traditional for men to be buried in a *tallit*, I have sometimes talked clients out of burying loved ones with it. Maybe they'll want to keep the *tallit* for a future occasion in the life of the family.

"My work is a *mitzvah* for me."

A funeral director's job description should include several elements that help in the imitation of God: The ability to help families create a funeral that gives honor and dignity to the deceased; the ability to help families choose the appropriate casket; the ability to comfort and deal with clients' fears. Sometimes there is the opportunity to imitate God by making *shalom* (peace) in a family. Sometimes, there is the opportunity to help people sort through their memories.

There is one other item on the list: Subtly teaching clients to intuit that there is a life beyond this life. As Jewish liturgy states: *Baruch attah Adonai, ha-noteah betocheinu chayei olam*, "Blessed is God who implants within us eternal life."

To be a conscientious funeral director is to help us redeem that which we must remember. It is necessary work; it is indispensable work; it is holy work.

Healing the Ill

"I, the Eternal, am your healer," God says to us (Ex. 15:26). This is the ultimate medical license. By healing, the doctor can imitate God, Who is the ultimate source of healing.

Abraham Joshua Heschel said, "Medicine is prayer in the form of a deed....The body is a sanctuary, the doctor is a priest....The act of healing is the highest form of the imitation of God."

As far back as the Middle Ages, medicine was the Jewish ticket into the wider world. It served as the best way for Jews to interact with gentile culture. In fact, an astonishingly large number of rabbis in the Middle Ages and the Renaissance were physicians. Not surprisingly, medical insights were often mingled with their more erudite discussions of Jewish law and practice. In the 12th century in Spain, for instance, Judah Ha Levi wrote: "Not upon my power of healing I rely/Only for Thine healing do I watch." In the 17th century in Ferrara, Italy, Rabbi Jacob Zahalon echoed one of the more sublime themes of Yom Kippur when he wrote: "Thou art the physician, not me. I am but clay in the Potter's hand, in the hand of the Creator of all things, and as the instrument through which You cure Your creatures."

In his biography of Maimonides, the great medieval philosopher, commentator and physician, Heschel noted that the great thinker spent his last years almost entirely engrossed in medicine. "This is Maimonides' last metamorphosis," Heschel wrote. "From metaphysics to medicine, from contemplation to practice, from speculation to the imitation of God. God is not only the object of knowledge; He is the example one is to follow."

I thought about Maimonides as I spoke with a young man in my congregation who wanted to become a plastic surgeon. He settled on this goal after working in an emergency room and seeing accident and burn victims who had been disfigured.

"I don't want to be a cosmetic plastic surgeon," he said. "I'm not interested in people's vanity. I want to help people who have real problems."

"There are many reasons people want to become doctors," I told him. "Some like the title or the status or the prestige. Some like the money. But the best reason I know is to be God's helper and aid those who are the victims of random misfortune in the world."

Beyond imitating God, the act of healing is, as Heschel says, an act of worship. In *How Can I Help?,* Paul Gorman and Ram Dass (formerly known as Richard Alpert) may have been thinking of those in the medical professions when they observed that "when we comfort a crying child, reassure a frightened patient, bring a glass of water to a bedridden elder, separateness dissolves and we are united in compassion." When we feel we are one with another person, we can sense what it feels to be one with God. At such moments, we are "vehicles of kindness, instruments of love. We feel transformed and connected to a deeper sense of identity." The human encounter transforms us, and lifts us to a higher place. Some call that place the very Throne of God.

Finding Routes to Holiness

Many aspects of the medical profession can be metaphors for all professionals in search of the holy in their work since *healing* is more than simply healing the body: It means anything we do that changes something for the better.

How can any of us find spirituality in the healing that might be part of our professions?

Humility

Some doctors feel God's presence not in what they *can* do, but paradoxically, in what they *cannot* do. Imitating God is not the same as *being* God. (Patients need to remember that, too.)

A few years ago, a female neonatologist in her early 30's told me, "I see my life as part of the divine fabric. But neonatology has helped me get in touch with my own humility. Its technology has advanced to the point where we can sustain a baby who is born at 23 weeks. The average baby is in the womb for about 36 weeks. But technology cannot sustain everyone. Neither can I. I am not God. There is a plan that we all fit into, and I cannot change what's not supposed to happen. Not everything is within my power."

The rediscovery of humility is one of the most significant

— and one of the most *Jewish* — trends in contemporary medical education. At a recent opening ceremony for medical students at Columbia University's College of Physicians and Surgeons, students donned their white coats and recited the Hippocratic Oath. During the ceremony, Dr. Linda Lewis, associate dean of student affairs, reminded the students that their white coats were "cloaks of compassion," symbols to remind them of the importance of humility in their careers. (Priests in the ancient Temple *also* wore white vestments to remind them of their finitude.) Similarly, at a recent Yale Medical School orientation session, professors told students, "Don't think that you're God. There is something beyond you."

I imagine that one of the *least* popular Talmudic passages in the corridors of the American Medical Association is: "The best of physicians are destined for hell." I once saw a doctor become furious when he heard a rabbi use that verse in a sermon. One interpretation of such a seemingly hostile phrase is that two sins — pride and murder — will send anyone who considers him or herself "the best of physicians" to hell. Such a physician might rely on personal judgement, not consult with another colleague, and, thus, harm a patient. As the Jewish theologian, Byron Sherwin, warned, "Both the life of the patient and the soul of the physician are constantly at risk."

Revelation

Physicians who specialize in medical research can meet God amid a joyous sense of discovery. That intellectual discovery is a refraction of the way God reveals truth to us.

After the Flood, according to a Talmudic legend, an angel brought Noah's son, Shem, to heaven where the remedies for every disease were revealed to him. Shem recorded these in a book, which he conveyed to Abraham, and which was transmitted from generation to generation, until it reached King Hezekiah of Judah in the eighth century B.C.E. The king suppressed the Book of Remedies because people were relying solely upon it for their healing, and, thus, divorcing God from the divine role of healer. Because the book was suppressed, all its medical insights had to be discovered again.

That legend teaches us that we must be part of the process of discovery, and that the answers to the most vexing medical problems of our time do not merely emerge from God's grace. Searching for the cure for a disease means seeking a revelation that was once given and is now lost, but is perhaps retrievable. Medical research becomes an act of higher Torah: A search for a text, an interpretation of that text, and engagement with that text. God "speaks" to us, once again — and we are able to go forth to heal.

Moreover, we find that sense of revelation in the struggle with ethical issues. A male internist in his early 30's told me that "God is present when *we* struggle with ethical decisions, and especially when we help patients and their families struggle with them. You can tell someone what you believe, but it's sometimes hard to give people absolutes. Ultimately, you can't make those decisions for others. You must be open to uncertainty at times. The very search for answers is the goal."

Covenant

A physician or nurse with a deep spiritual life understands that there is a *covenant* between him or her and the patient. This is a triangular covenant in which God is the vortex. Implicit in this covenant is the idea that physicians must treat patients as being made in the image of God, as souls as well as bodies. This notion of covenant should infuse our relationships with clients and customers, as well as patients.

As Martin Buber might say, we should learn to treat people as "Thous" rather than "Its." A friend of mine who is a professor of nursing has said: "It is important for my nursing students to see that their patients have spiritual needs. It is important for me to intermittently stop us from our relentless task-oriented work and really look at these people we are treating. How can we address the patients' striving to make sense of their experiences and to find meaning and a place in the scheme of things?"

Years ago, I knew someone who wanted to go to medical school. He was a true misanthrope: He simply didn't like people. He chose surgery as his specialty because, as he rationalized, "The patient is asleep. It's just a body. I don't need any bedside manner." Happily, years of medical school made him more sensitive — and turned him into a better doctor.

My friend was not alone in his assumptions about his role in the medical profession. Lucrative "no patient contact" specialties like anesthesiology and radiology have become increasingly popular in the last decade. In response to doctors who retreat into this sanitized medical world, the 19th century

Hasidic rebbe, Nachman of Breslov, said that the true healer must have true spiritual depth and not be a "mechanic" of the body. Physicians who neglected their own or their *patients'* spirituality were virtually sorcerers trying to manipulate natural forces for their own self-aggrandizement.

Heschel believed that "we cannot speak about the patient as a person unless we also probe the meaning of the doctor as a person. You can only sense a person if you are a person. Being a person depends upon being alive to the wonder and mystery that surround us, upon the realization that there is no ordinary man. Every man is an extraordinary man....The doctor is not only a healer of disease; he is also a source of emanation of the spirit of concern and compassion. The doctor may be a saint without knowing it and without pretending to be one."

Yet, it is important for us to understand that *saintliness does not imply perfection.* The doctor may say: "I'm *not* Albert Schweitzer. What if I became a doctor because I want to make a lot of money, or because my ego wanted me to become a doctor?" Fine. Continue to heal people and save lives. Healing is the gateway to saintliness. Perhaps your soul will catch up with what your hands are already doing.

Saintliness comes even in the little things. A former nursing home administrator told me that he believed that everyone at his facility — doctors, nurses, even orderlies — had roles in healing and in providing hope. He directed his custodial staff to speak to patients whenever they cleaned a room.

"It helped the patients," he remarked. "But more than that, it helped the custodians. It made them feel that they were part of the care process. It gave them a true sense of nobility."

The Encounter with the God of Life and Death

At those moments when the fragility of life is revealed anew to us, the act of healing truly becomes an act of prayer.

A friend of mine, an internist in his early 40's, recently said to me: "We find God at the borders and boundaries of life and death, and of health and illness. When things are great, fine. God comes in when there's trouble. While grappling with the meaning of pain, I've been sustained by my belief that a suffering patient goes on to an afterlife. I believe that people live on in some way, even physically and genetically through having children.

"I will never forget the loving presence of the family and friends of a 10-year-old boy dying of a brain tumor. Through them, I felt God's Presence. It confirmed my belief in God. Nature cannot create such a moment. Only God."

As my friend was telling me this, I thought of the Talmudic saying that when the soul leaves the body, it makes a sound that can be heard around the world and is echoed throughout the cosmos. God is in those moments. This is more than a body dying, or the result of a failed operation or the terminus of a terminal illness. This is a *soul* leaving the body, its corporal home.

Hope

Finally, doctors or nurses must be active agents of faith, courage — and, mostly, of hope. Philosopher Peter Berger wrote in his classic book, *A Rumor of Angels,* that our ability to hope is one of the most important "proofs" that there is a God. Judaism so profoundly believes in hope that no scriptural reading in synagogue can end on a negative note. Physicians must bring this same message of hope into all that they do. As a doctor in my congregation once said during a workshop on spirituality, "When someone survives an illness, that is the hand of God. I believe that. Faith helps in ways that we cannot know."

Those of us in *this* world must become active agents of a hope that transcends us. Healing means that we refuse to accept the world as it is. According to the modern Orthodox theologian Rabbi Irving Greenberg, a primitive view of the world "sees nature as imbued with untouchable sacredness or as the incarnation of gods who must be bought off but never challenged....When people accept the world as it is, poverty and sickness are the human condition."

"Tampering" with the World to Better It

Judaism teaches that humans should use the world — and change it. As Genesis commanded, "Fill the earth and conquer it, work it and protect it." Judaism is not pantheism. It does not believe that the entire world is God. In fact, precisely because the world is *not* God, we can tamper with it and make it better. We are not passive puppets in the hands of fate.

I once taught this idea to a group of adults. Over a cup of coffee, after the seminar, a young man approached me.

"I work as an emergency medical technician," he said. "Occasionally, my beeper goes off at three o'clock in the morning because someone is very sick or injured. It means that I have to go mess around with *karma,* with fate; I have to go and tamper with the world."

Tampering with the world to make it better is holy work.

One way to tamper with the world is *prayer.* Judaism has a long, rich tradition of praying for a sick person's recovery. The Talmud records instances when people visited the sick, and their personal presence was sufficient to heal.

Sadly, many doctors forget to bring their *own* spirituality to their offices and on their hospital rounds. Presumably, they think that mixing traditional medicine and prayer would be as *improper* as mixing government and religion. In *Healing Words: The Power of Prayer and the Practice of Medicine,* Dr. Larry Dossey cites scientific studies that prayer has more healing power than we had thought — when it is combined with modern medical treatments. Such empirical studies demonstrate that religious faith "works" in a way that we might have once rejected as being irrational, and that when we pray for people who are ill — *and when they know that they are the focus of that prayer* — the healing process is aided.

Prayer must be considered seriously as a therapeutic device. While the doctor or nurse may not want to impose his or her religious beliefs on a patient, "long distance prayer" for a patient can work. That might mean prayer in a synagogue or church. The ancient rabbis said that when a person visits the sick, that visit removes one-60th of the illness. There may, in fact, be some truth in that since recent studies reveal that personal presence and love can heal. The body and the soul are much closer to each other than we think, and almost as close as religion would have us believe.

According to the Talmud, when Rav Huna asked his son why he had not studied with the sage Rav Hisda, Rabbah replied, "Why should I study with him? He only lectures on secular matters, like health and hygiene." To which his father scolded: "Rav Hisda lectures on health and hygiene and you call it secular matters! All the more reason why you should attend his lectures!"

These are not secular matters. Some say that attending a lecture on health and hygiene is yet another way to learn about God. Some say that it is the best mini-course on theology there is.

Sanctifying the Creative Impulse

The paradigmatic act of creation is, of course, God's creation of the universe. It is interesting to note, then, that the first thing that Jews collectively created for themselves after the liberation from bondage in Egypt was the ancient desert tabernacle. Yet God was constantly implicated in that human act. God gave explicit directions regarding its design, even to the extent of showing Moses a blueprint of how it should look. Just as God rested from the labors of creation, so, too, construction on the tabernacle ceased on Shabbat. To have a place to worship God, Jews had to mimic God's creativity. According to the ancient rabbis, God's presence dwelled among us only *after* we had engaged in that creative work. This was God's way of saying that the Jewish people had come of age, that they were ready to have a place for the beginning of a long and intimate conversation with God.

The chief architect of the tabernacle was named Bezalel, which means "in the shadow of God." His name survives in the Bezalel Academy of Arts and Design, Israel's pre-eminent art school. The name "Bezalel" embraces the paradox: Our creativity is an imitation of God. But it is *only* an imitation, only a *shadow* of God's supernal creativity.

A friend of mine who has been a weaver and ceramicist for 20 years is well aware of this relation between her craft and her faith: "For the first 15 years I was an artist, I had to constantly struggle for new ideas. Ending a work was like a mini-death. Once I finished something, I never knew if I would be able to create again. When I began putting God and Judaism into my art, it gave me a sense of my renewed faith, and I would create with greater ease. Ideas began to come without struggle."

"I learned that I needed to listen to God. I felt a sense of partnership with the side of God that is within us and also with the external side of God. My art has become a way to combine the *shekhinah* [the interior, female, quieter side of God] and the external, masculine, out-in-the-world God."

Her weaving, she said, "is particularly spiritual. The warp [the vertical threads] is the *is,* that which is there. The weft [what you throw into it] represents the act of choosing your life path. A common theme in the spirituality of weaving is that in every object you weave, there must be a mistake. That belief may go back to an ancient fear that the gods may be enraged if you are too perfect."

For some religious feminists, weaving has become a spiritual metaphor. In one of her poems, the poet Adrienne Rich speaks of finding an old piece of her grandmother's patchwork which was never finished, and what it means to pick up the work where her grandmother had left off. Religion also is a tapestry created of traditions, memories, songs, poems, stories, visions, and values.

Constructing a Bridge of Meaning

Creativity, obviously, goes far beyond the visual artist. An Orthodox architect once told me that he had many complex design problems and challenges. "I can go a week without solving a particular problem well," he said. "But then, after saying my evening prayers and going to bed, I will visually see the completed problem in its entirety. Oddly enough, this never happens on Shabbat."

This architect has a vision of the completed project, just like the vision of the tabernacle that God gave Moses. That act of revelation never happens on Shabbat, just as the creation of the tabernacle ceased on Shabbat.

So there are numerous bridges, back and forth, between art and religion. Art and religion have common tasks: To find meaning, patterns and coherence in life.

When we realize that the significance of what we do with

our hands leads us beyond our selves, we realize that something connects us to the life of the cosmos itself.

As one artist told me: "I find myself going through the seven days of creation when I create. First, there is the need to create, but there is also chaos at the beginning. You hover over your work, just like God did. Then comes the concept, which is the mundane equivalent of 'Let there be light.' As the idea becomes illuminated, you find the form for it. And then you say, 'This is good,' just as God said upon the creation of the world. Since we are created in God's image, we also participate in that great act of creation. Reading Psalms in the morning helps my own creativity. It helps me think of myself as being like God, as *mechadesh b'kol yom*, as one that renews and creates every day."

Being Like God

In a wonderful pun found in the Midrash, *Ha-tzur*, God the Rock, becomes *Ha-Tzayar*, the Divine Artist. In the Midrash, God is called an architect, Whose blueprint for creation was the Torah itself. The Torah is the way that God wants the world to look. When God fears that Adam and Eve will eat from the Tree of Knowledge and, therefore, become like God, Rashi, the medieval commentator, suggests that to be like God is to be creators of worlds. When we are creators, we are most like God. It is not an usurpation: It is fulfillment.

Understand, then: These are *imitators of God*: Artists, musicians, choreographers, sculptors, playwrights, architects, builders and designers. In our time, computer programmers are God-imitators, creating entire binary, microchip-driven universes. In *The Soul of a New Machine,* Tracy Kidder described the feelings of those who had just built a new computer: "Many looked around for words to describe their true reward. They used such phrases as 'self-fulfillment,' 'a feeling of accomplishment,' 'self-satisfaction'....Ninety-eight percent of the thrill comes from knowing that the thing you designed works, and works almost the way you expected it would. If that happens, part of *you* is in that machine." This is no different, I suspect, from God looking at the Divine handiwork, and finding it "very good."

Think about it this way. Anyone in the repair business is an imitator of God. A carpenter in Jerusalem helped in the restoration of Nachman of Breslov's chair, which the Breslover Hasidim had smuggled out of the Ukraine, piece by piece. He describes his work this way: "Reb Nachman himself taught about the importance of failure and getting back up. It's the way the world works. The world is imperfect and it is up to us to fix it. So, I restore things."

Our Creativity Gives Birth to the World — Again

In a mystical teaching, Enoch, a minor character from the early chapters of Genesis, is transformed into a shoemaker. He utters these words from the *Shema* whenever he fixes shoes: "Blessed is God's glorious kingdom forever and ever." He believed that, while stitching the seams on his shoes, he was imitating God: He saw in every stitch a way to unify and connect all the cosmic worlds. Enoch checked every thread to see that it was whole. He worked with a sense of responsibility for the integrity of his product, and in so doing he achieved divine unification.

This kind of thinking will help us heal much of the sadness of today's world, a world in which meaning has been dissipated by technology. Too often, the manual worker's task has been reduced to a single repetitive, monotonous act. About 200 years ago, almost everyone worked with their hands and created with their hands. When a person made a pair of shoes, they were born in the mind, and became real in the hands and in the shop. For a fleeting moment, the craftsperson or repairperson could feel a sense of what it meant to be God.

In their desire to repair the world, scientists are also God-imitators. The late Rabbi Joseph Soloveitchik, the sage of modern Orthodoxy, implied this in his classic essay, *Halachic Man:* "Scientific curiosity and the desire to bring order and control into the cosmos are grounded in the Judaic principle to imitate God." Recently Dr. Daniel Cohen, a French Jew who is one of the world's leading geneticists, explained his involvement in the human genome project in Jewish terms: "*Kabbalah* [Jewish mysticism] speaks of repairing the world. Our job is to correct nature's imperfections. For me, working on the genome project helps to repair the world."

A woman poet and playwright described her creativity to me differently: "To me, the creative process is like childbirth. Going into a room where one of my plays was being produced gave me a tremendous visceral physical release. I thought, 'Thank God. I couldn't have carried those ten characters around with me anymore.' They had just exploded out of me."

In the traditional view of creation, God *speaks* the world into being: "God said, 'Let there be light,' and there was light." But the contemporary theologian Arthur Green has noticed that Jewish mysticism teaches that the world is *born,* not *spoken,* out of God. This birth is associated with the Hebrew letter *hey,* that twice appears in the four-letter divine name, *yud hey vav hey. Hey* "is associated with the inner divine womb and the act of birth," states Green. "This face of God is that of primal mother, the divine as life giver, as nourishing and sustaining source. It is from this God-womb that all variety is born."

Many people who find creativity in their work echo the observation that Godliness is revealed by *giving birth* to a project or program, and that God is present in the awe of that moment.

Bringing God into our work means seeing creative potential in all that we do. It is how we recapitulate creation itself.

Emulating Divine Competence

Competence is part of the covenant that God made with each of us. That covenant does not begin or end with us. It begins in the Garden of Eden itself, and it ends only with the coming of the Messianic Age. God creates us to be creators and transformers.

The first chapter of Genesis states that "God created man

in His image....Male and female He created them. God blessed them and God said to them, 'Be fertile and increase, fill the earth and master it; and rule the fish of the sea, the birds of the sky, and all the living things that creep on earth.'"

Adam was made in the divine image. He was given the task of procreating and dominating the earth. In the words of Rabbi Joseph B. Soloveitchik, Adam — who is us — is creative, enamored of technology, and seeks dignity by mastering and transforming nature. He is a problemsolver and an entrepreneur, aggressive and bold. He builds, plants, harvests, regulates rivers, heals the sick and governs. Every time he steps back and looks at what he has accomplished, he imitates God who evaluated the divine handiwork at the end of each stage of creation.

The way of competence is the way of the business world. Business is not only the land of the bottom line. It is also the realm of imagination, planning and doing. As a young entrepreneur in the food business told me, "I find spirituality in my business through dreaming, envisioning, planning, finding partners for my visions, and then creating something that wasn't there before." Philosophers would call that creation *ex nihilo,* creating something out of nothing — just as God did in Genesis. In the business world, spiritual moments can be as heady as the pause from the work of creation in which God says, "This is very good." The business and financial world is also the arena for the imitation of God.

In the Yom Kippur liturgy, God is called the Divine Potter Who must work with defective human material. We are like

God. Whenever we try to create something in our work, we realize that we work with less than perfect human materials. Some people have used the "artistic" metaphor to talk about human resource management.

But which form of art is it? Some say that management is like sculpture, trying to transform people and program into a particular vision. Others say it is closer to dance, for we work with living, breathing artists-in-their-own-right who have their own unique talents and temperaments.

Imitating by Omission: Making Room for Others in the World

Competence is the will of God. Soul-searching is the will of God. Sometimes the way we imitate God is not in what we *do*, but in what we do *not* do.

The dominant figure in the spiritual life of 16th century Safed, a city in northern Israel with a long spiritual tradition, was Isaac Luria. He was born in Jerusalem in 1534. After being orphaned at an early age, he lived in Cairo with a rich uncle. As a young man, he intensely studied mysticism and lived as a hermit, one of the few in Jewish history. He married, had a family, and moved to Safed, where a small circle of students gathered around him. Within three years, he created a radical new way of thinking about the world, about suffering, about evil and postulated a new Jewish creation epic.

Before the creation of the world, said Luria, all was filled with God's light. When it was time to create the world, there was no room for it, because God fills all space. To make room, God had to contract. That contraction is called *tzimtzum.*

We may consider the injunction to imitate God as a commandment to be competent and assertive. But another way to imitate God is to imitate *tzimtzum*: Sometimes competence demands that we step back and let *others* do and be. We see this in parents, who must step back to let their children grow. We see it in teachers, who must often relinquish their sense of self so students can meet new challenges. We see it in managers who must step back and let people do what they do best, even if that means they fail.

As the entrepreneur in the food business told me, "I hope someday to be able to step back totally and let my workers really take over the business. Then, I'll find something else to do." He said this to me with utter security — and with a palpable love for his employees.

Such humility is desirable in our jobs. John McCormack, author of *What They Don't Teach You At Harvard Business School,* recommends that all executives have certain words on their lips: "I don't know." "I need help." "I was wrong." "Thank you." Such words are about the withdrawal of omnipotence, of personal power, of our *tzimtzum* mirroring God's *tzimtzum.*

A woman minister recently learned this difficult lesson during a brief stint as a temporary secretary in a medical office. After an especially trying day, the doctor said, "I must be driving you crazy!"

"No," she answered. "From 8:30 to 5:00, what you want is what I want. After that, you're on your own. But while I'm here, my job is to do things the way you want them."

Later, reflecting on the incident, she said, "One mark of success will be that I am not remembered, that there is a neat filing system in place which anyone can use, that the manuscripts I type are so clear that they can be published without effort, that the people who need to talk to my doctors are able to do so with minimal interference from me. For me to be successful at my job, I have to lay aside my 'self,' the ego that demands recognition and turf and something uniquely my own."

It takes an enormously secure sense of self to be able to do that. As our young food entrepreneur has said, "I get excited when I see people grow and reach their potential. I want to help my business grow to the point where it can be run without me. I ultimately want to remove myself from it."

In Hasidic thought, putting one's self on hold is called *bittul ha-yesh,* literally, "the annihilation of substance." It means: I must withdraw from my ego needs, just as God withdrew in creating the world.

Whatever else God is, God is *very* secure. Such confidence is not such a bad thing to imitate.

Erecting Altars — Even in the Office

To some of us, the very idea of imitating God may seem farfetched, or arrogant. We may prefer our spirituality to be somewhere else — "up there" in the stars or "in here" in the soul. But the world of spirituality is not only in the soul or in the cosmos. *It is in one's very hands.*

This simple yet powerful truth might give us a new reason to wake up in the morning, get dressed, start the car or catch the bus or train. Knowing that you can imitate God in your work, let us transform the office into a sanctuary.

God called the Jewish people to be "a kingdom of priests."

Most of us have more sanctuaries and altars in our midst than we can name. Like the priests of yore, we must remember that we can kindle fires wherever we go.

By doing so, we will understand that, like the fire on the ancient altar, this fire, too, will never be extinguished.

Making It Real in Your Life

- ***How do you imitate God in your work? Do you "clothe the naked"? Do you comfort others? In what ways are you called upon to heal? Does your work let you be creative?***
- ***When have you had moments when, like God, you have found your work to be "very good"?***
- ***When have you felt most competent in your work?***
- ***When have you found yourself imitating God by being less competent, by engaging in* tzimtzum*?***
- ***When have you felt humility, rather than grandeur, in your work?***
- ***What can you do differently when you next go to work?***

Four

Being God's Partner

"Human beings are God's language."
— *Hasidic saying*

One of the best-known Jewish folk expressions is *chutzpah.* It has several translations: "Boldness," "nerve," "gall," "arrogance." But *chutzpah* is a theological term, as well. It describes a little-known aspect of our relationship with God: Something along the lines of "spiritual audacity." *Chutzpah* is Abraham challenging God to spare the evil cities of Sodom and Gomorrah; *chutzpah* is Job challenging God's justice; *chutzpah* is the Yiddish Holocaust poet Kadya Molodovsky crying out, "O God of mercy, choose another people. We are tired of death, tired of corpses. We have no more prayers."

The last chapter discussed imitating God in our careers. Some might think that this is *chutzpah.* It's not. It's just part of the moral vocabulary that every Jew has inherited from past generations. It simply means *doing what God does.*

Picking Up Where God Left Off

Let me introduce you to a theological first cousin of imitating God: *Being God's partner.* Whereas imitating God means "doing what God does," being God's partner means *picking up where God left off.* On the seventh day, God rested and said, "It [creation] is very good."

Good, but not perfect. This very powerful God needs *us* to be a partner in the unfolding, incomplete pieces of creation. We are not, therefore, insignificant specks in the cosmos. We are nobility. President John F. Kennedy unwittingly paraphrased Jewish theology when he suggested in his 1961 inaugural address that "God's work on earth must truly be our own."

God-partnership is one of the great hidden themes of Jewish literature, life and lore. Take ritual, for example. When Jews circumcise their infant sons eight days after birth, they become God's partners by completing the act of creation: They "complete" the little boy by bringing him into the covenant.

When a Jew recites *kiddush* (the blessing over wine at the beginning of Shabbat), he or she states, "Now the heavens were completed — and the earth and all that is within them." Raising the Kiddush cup and proclaiming the creation potentially transforms the worshipper into a partner of God. Some hold the Kiddush cup with their fingers pointed aloft in the shape of the Hebrew letter *shin*, which stands for one of God's names, Shaddai. This helps us remember that our hands can be the hands of God in this world.

By giving thanks for food, we affirm that we are partners with God. We can't recite *motzi* (the blessing over bread) over wheat or recite *kiddush* over a cluster of grapes. Wheat and grapes come from God, but *humans* must transform them into bread and wine. It would be wonderful if bread grew on trees or wine flowed from rivers. But that's not how the world works. To eat, to drink, to live and flourish, we must actively participate as partners in the ongoing process of creation and bringing God's work to perfection.

Torah itself is an act of human-divine partnership. When Moses saw the Israelites dancing around the Golden Calf, he shattered the Tablets of the Law. The set that replaced these was different than the old one: Moses and God *together* made it. Moses carved the tablets; God wrote the words. Judaism is an act of human-divine partnership: God writes (or inspires) the words; Jews interpret and live them.

True, the idea of God-partnership can seem pretentious or presumptuous. As the late Reform rabbi, Bernard J. Bamberger, said: "A youngster just admitted to partnership in a big law office would be ill-advised to say to the head of the firm, 'I'm glad to have you as my partner.'" It is more accurate to say that we are God's *junior* partners. This means that we live in covenant with God and that God is interested in us and invested in our existence, just as we are invested in *God's* existence. Our dilemma and our goal is to assure that this partnership with God brings nobility to our work, purpose to our livelihood and deep satisfaction to our labors.

Let's look at some examples.

Seeking Justice: The Way of Lawyers

We should all seek justice in what we do. In the legal profession, almost everyone wants to become a partner in a law firm. But as the Talmud states, "Every judge who renders a fair decision is like a partner of the Holy One in the act of creation" (Talmud, *Shabbat* 119b). The Talmud also promises that "a judge who decides a case in accordance with true equity causes the *Shekhinah,* God's Presence, to dwell in the midst of Israel."

Understand what this can mean to your inner life as a lawyer or judge. By seeking justice, you share in divine power. You can bring God into the world. *Failing* to bring justice into the world *also* has cosmic implications, for lawlessness drives God's presence into exile.

Lawyers or judges can find God in their careers by discerning *how God would want us to behave in this world.* This is a quintessentially Jewish task, and perhaps the height of divine partnership.

Eskimos supposedly have 30 words for "snow." This is a fallacy. But if they did, Jews would have only slightly *fewer* words for "justice": *Din, tzedek* and *mishpat,* among others, each with a slightly different nuance. The prophet Hosea imagined God saying these words that have become part of the Jewish wedding ceremony: "I betroth you [the Jewish people] to Me in righteousness (*tzedek*), and in justice (*mishpat*) and in lovingkindness (*hesed*) and in mercy (*rachamim*)." Our relationship with God is predicated on those principles. Ancient legend states that there are two thrones in heaven: Justice and mercy. On Yom Kippur, God shuttles back and forth between them. God needs our help in balancing justice and mercy in the world.

As Haim Cohen, the late chief justice of Israel's Supreme Court, said: "God in divine wisdom instilled in every human being a sense of justice and a sense of injustice to serve as the test to which all justice and injustice must be put."

Empathy and Repentance: Pathways to God

Lawyers or judges can *echo God's empathy*, as can each of us in our own work. As a friend of mine who is a senior judge said, "One of the great spiritual experiences in my law career occurred when I heard a woman with an abusive husband crying in Family Court. When I heard her cry, I silently said, 'God, where are You? How can you let such things happen?'"

But God has not forgotten us. One of the missions God has given us is to heal the injustice of the world. God is so singularly *obsessed* with justice that we have been commanded "not [to] mistreat any widow or orphan. If you do mistreat them, I will heed their outcry as soon as they cry out to Me" (Ex. 22:21-22). The basic linchpin of Jews' moral imagination is that God heard the cries of the Jewish people in Egypt — and that God hears the cries of the oppressed today wherever they may be.

My judge friend wept when he saw injustice. God wept with him. Doing justice for widows and orphans means doing justice for some of the most vulnerable people in society. It means being a partner with God in assuring justice in this world.

Lawyers or judges should know that their actions reflect upon God. If God cares about justice, then the way we administer justice implicates God.

A friend, a Jewish lawyer, once told me, "I deal a lot with Christian clients. When I do so, I'm always aware that I represent the Jewish people as well. I want to make sure that my actions reflect well on us."

"You're right," I said. "You should act in a way that brings credit to the Jewish people. But let's go beyond sociology to theology. Jews care deeply about how they appear to non-Jews. But they need to also care about how they appear to God. God cares about what we do, even when non-Jews don't know or don't care about our actions."

Lawyers and judges can hear God's voice by being agents of inner change and growth. Judaism calls this *teshuvah,* or repentance.

A lawyer in his early 40's once told me, "I find spirituality by seeing my clients change their ways. Sometimes when I work with a client who is clearly guilty, I say, 'You're at a point in your life where you can make a choice. You can continue on the road you're on. If you do, you're doomed to terrible failure. Or, you can clean up your act.'

"Sometimes, I get a postcard from them a few years later telling me that they've gone straight and found a job. It gives me a wonderful feeling deep inside."

That feeling is God's Presence, back at home in the world,

redeemed from its exile. It's the presence of a God Who wants us to collaborate in moving people towards a higher, better vision of themselves.

Being God's Partner by Making Peace

We all can hear the voice of God by seeking *shalom* (peace) through conflict resolution. By doing this, we become the counterpart of Aaron, who was Judaism's first priest and the brother of Moses. Jewish lore says that Aaron went back and forth between enemies, saying to each one, "So-and-so feels terrible about what is going on, and begs your forgiveness."

Aaron was the *rodef shalom*, the seeker of peace par excellence in the Jewish tradition. The recent growth in divorce mediation, which helps people resolve potentially difficult situations through non-litigational negotiation, echoes those voices in society that want to be Aarons, seekers of peace.

Judges and lawyers can find spirituality in humility. As one retired judge told me, "A plaque in my office bears the words of the prophet Micah: 'To do justice, and to love mercy, and to walk humbly with thy God.' When I am successful in dealing with people, I realize that there is another intervening agent beyond myself. That's God. I have had many difficult decisions in my career. At those times, I call upon divine guidance."

Finally, judges and lawyers can know that God finishes their work for them. True justice is essentially transcendent. As Deuteronomy (1:17) says, "You shall not fear any man, for true judgement is God's."

After years of controversy and some reasonable doubt, in 1993, Israel's Supreme Court finally acquitted John Demjanuk of being the infamous Ivan the Terrible, a sadistic guard at the death camp of Treblinka. In its final opinion, the court included this elegant, quintessentially Jewish statement: "The matter is over, but not finished. The truth is beyond the knowledge of any human judge."

Years ago, I worked as a part-time Jewish chaplain in a prison. To know the real meaning of sin and atonement, redemption and reconciliation, try praying with people who have *really* sinned. Despite my initial trepidations, I came to like the hoodlums, petty thieves, white-collar criminals, and even the one infamous murderer who formed my little congregation.

When my friends asked "How can you work with those guys?", I said, "A human judge has already judged them, so they don't need me to be their judge. I am their counselor and teacher. In ways that we cannot know, God will ultimately judge them as well."

Being Partners in the Work of Repair: The Way of Therapists

According to the kabbalist Isaac Luria, when God contracted to make room for the creation of the world, divine light flowed into cosmic vessels. But, in a great cosmic catastrophe, the vessels shattered and divine sparks dispersed throughout all existence.

Yet, the sparks were *not* irretrievably lost. We can find them: Through prayer and religious study, through each deed of kindness and justice that we perform. This is called *tikkun olam*, repairing the world. Potentially, every holy act we do can repair the world. When the world is sufficiently repaired, it will be ready for the Messianic Age. In the words of *Aleinu*, the great liturgical summation of Jewish striving and purpose, *L'taken olam b'malchut shaddai*, "We must perfect the world under the reign of the Almighty."

The Jews of 16th century Safed in Israel were exiles from their beloved Spain, which had expelled them in 1492. They constructed a theology that spoke to the reality of their exile. As Isaac Luria said, "We are in exile. Our exile is part of the broken nature of existence itself. Even God is in exile from the world."

"But we are not powerless," he said. "We have nobility. We can find the sparks of the holy that are in the world. We can lift up the sparks. It is like stirring up the ashes in a fireplace. You poke the ashes, and the sparks that are hidden there fly upwards. What we do in our lives is crucial for the welfare of the cosmos. We can repair the world. And we can even repair the rift that exists between God and the world."

What does it mean to be God's partner in the work of *tikkun*? And what does it mean to bring that act of *tikkun* into our work?

Ever since Sigmund Freud, gallons of ink have been spilled on the connections between Judaism and psychoanalysis, psychotherapy, psychiatry, psychology, social work, and other facets of the helping professions.

Some find the roots of psychoanalysis in Joseph's interpretation of Pharaoh's dreams in Egypt, and, centuries later, in Daniel's interpretation of King Nebuchadnezzar's dreams in Babylon. Some see the invention of psychotherapy as another example of how Jews have de novo created an entirely new endeavor, just as they created the American garment industry virtually out of nothing.

Therapy, psychoanalysis, social work and counselling can all be vehicles to being God's partner in repair. Those in these helping professions help the hurt and the injured and the confused restore wholeness and harmony to their lives. The mystics of Safed knew that when we repair the self, we mirror the potential repair of the world. Such repair is simultaneously creative and reconstructive. Sometimes therapy means helping clients understand that the empty places inside are where God can reside. As a therapist told me, "People who are addicted, whether to drugs, alcohol, binge eating, sex or shopping, all report feelings of emptiness. If you ask them where that emptiness is, they point to their hearts. That emptiness is the lack of God in their lives."

Just as the theologian Martin Buber taught, when we have a genuine encounter with each other, God is present. A therapist in his early 40's told me, "Therapy is basically a relationship between two people. When I have that relationship in therapy, I feel God's presence."

"I once worked with a 16-year-old boy," he said. "His mother warned me that I could never form a relationship with him because he doesn't form relationships with people. The first time we met, he was very angry and only stayed with me for half a minute. The second time he could only stay a minute. After awhile, he was able to stay for ten minutes. Those ten minutes grew until we had a relationship. When that bond exists and genuine healing takes place, I feel that God is present in the room."

Therapy, psychoanalysis, social work, and counselling recapitulate the Jewish story. The healing each offers is the psychological equivalent of redemption from Egypt. Egypt is not just a geographical place. It is a metaphor for enslavement and bondage. The Hebrew word for Egypt, *Mitzrayim*, is in the plural form. There are many Egypts. Every person who is psychologically enslaved is in Egypt.

Therapy is also *revelation*. During the therapeutic process, we stand at the foot of an inner Sinai for a moment of self-awareness. It is also the living extension of the act of revelation: Interpretation.

In *The Interpretation of Dreams*, Freud remarked that dreams were "like sacred texts." Each of us is a holy text, a sacred collection of layers of stories, images, symbols — and of their accumulated interpretations and re-interpretations. As a Reform rabbi, Rachel Mikva, said, "The act of counselling becomes the sharing of human texts. By listening to, and caring about, the client's story, by responding to the person who tells it, the counselor is empathetic. The counselor is a *more derech* [a teacher of the journey], showing the way toward new interpretations, new possibilities for meaning."

Finally, therapy can reflect the dominant theme of Jewish history in exile: The ability to rebuild after destruction. Jews have proven to the world that the human soul can rise above pain. As a Hasidic saying goes, "If you want to find a spark, you must sift through the ashes."

When the Babylonians destroyed the First Temple in 586 B.C.E., Jews returned from exile and rebuilt it. When the Romans destroyed Judean independence in 70 C.E., a new Judaism was born, a Judaism of prayer, *mitzvot* and Torah study as sacred acts that connect the worshipper to God. As we have seen, when the Jews were expelled from Spain in 1492, they created a mysticism that gave meaning to their exile. After the devastating Chmielnitzky massacres in the Ukraine in 1648, Hasidism, a revolution in the inner life of the Jew, was born. After the Holocaust, the State of Israel was born, the survivors of the Shoah built new lives, and the American Jewish community came to maturity.

These are all acts of re-building, of seeing what is left and making the remnants sing. Therapy can be like that, as well. As a former occupational therapist reflected, "I find that my Jewish identity had a lot to do with being an occupational therapist. Occupation therapists are adapters. We try to find ways for patients to return to the activities that were important in their lives without holding out false hopes. My relationship with God is like that. You need to cut through the extraneous to get to the core of what it means to have a relationship with the Eternal One."

Bringing Strength to the Frail: Caring for the Aged

After Moses shattered the first Tablets of the Law, he put their fragments into the Ark, along with the new, rewritten Tablets. The Israelites carried those fragments through the wilderness; the sanctity of the shattered tablets did not vanish the moment they broke.

That story teaches us how to treat the elderly. Jewish lore sometimes calls the elderly "broken tablets." Despite their frailty, perhaps even their brokenness, they are irreducibly holy. Whoever works in restoring the fragile elderly to wholeness is a partner with God.

Years ago, my synagogue opened its doors to a Parkinson's Disease support group. Several times a week, elderly Parkinson's patients crowd the halls. It is not always the most uplifting sight; many congregants would probably rather see healthy, beautiful nursery school children running around the synagogue building. But whenever I worry about that, I remind myself of the story of the broken tablets — and give thanks that my synagogue is trying to glue the *living* tablets back together again.

A woman in Miami in her early 50's who works with the aged told me, "When I started working with the elderly, I said to myself that I am getting paid for being me and for doing what I would have done as a volunteer for free. My work brings support and dignity to frail elderly people and Alzheimer's patients. I have one mission: To acknowledge the dignity of every living being.

"The concept of 'doing God's work'," she continued, "is not only a Christian idea. When you work with the elderly, you are truly doing God's work on a nine-to-five basis. We can't just park our religious faith at the doors of our workplaces and offices. In the extreme, that kind of religious `parking' brought on the Third Reich, because many Nazis acted completely contrary to how their religious faith would have had them behave. My work lets me bring my passions, values, and religious vision into the public square and into the marketplace."

When people do work that is a *mitzvah,* their labors can restore and transform the soul. A woman in Florida in her 40's switched from being a "high powered" executive in the banking industry to caring for the elderly. She founded Compassionate Companions, which provides the elderly with companions who cook for them, read for them, play cards with them, drive them to social events or to doctors and shop for them.

"It happened by accident, though perhaps not *really* by accident," she said. "I am the oldest grandchild of a Hasidic grandmother. She used to take care of the older people in the neighborhood. When she was 88, she would take two streetcars to bring home baked goods to an old-age home. When she got very sick, people came out of the woodwork to visit her and say goodbye. My grandmother was a true part of my being.

"About seven years ago, I had an emergency appendectomy. The night after my surgery, I dreamed of my grandmother. In the dream, she said, 'I will watch over you, and one day you will watch over old people just like I did.'

"Soon after that, I realized that I wanted to do something

more altruistic and less 'bottom-line' with my life. I left banking. When a friend asked me to help with her dying grandfather, I started making him chicken soup and brisket. Suddenly, this old man was no longer dying. I decided that I would find *other* people who want a mission in life. I would teach them to care for older people at home and provide medicine for the soul."

Her work is not always easy or rewarding. Like Isaac Luria and the mystics of Safed, she constructs meaning from brokenness. "Even when things don't go well, I feel that I can learn a lesson. When I have a negative experience with a client or a worker, I learn that the problems are as valuable as the good stuff. It's like being in a relationship with God. That relationship is not always so wonderful, either."

She, also, is a partner with God.

Suddenly, life is very different. It is no longer prosaic. It is now a love poem to God and to existence itself.

What a joyful paradox: This powerful God that *we* need, needs *us*.

Desperately.

Making It Real in Your Life

- ***Have you ever felt that you were God's partner?***
- ***When in your work have you sought justice?***

- *When have you sought* shalom*?*
- *How, in your work, are you a partner in the task of world-repair? How can you begin to be a partner in world-repair?*
- *Have you helped someone achieve wholeness? Are there ways in your work for you to do this?*
- *When have you felt that your own life story was retelling the story of your people?*

Five

Standing in the Presence of God: *How to Hear God's Voice in Business Ethics*

"Adonai, who may abide in Your house?....
Those who are upright; who do justly; who speak the truth within their hearts. Who do not slander others, or wrong them, or bring shame upon them.
Who scorn the lawless, but honor those who revere God.
Who give their word, and, come what may, do not retract.
Who do not exploit others, who never take bribes.
Those who live in this way shall never be shaken.
— *Psalm 15*

A religious trivia question, that turns out not to be trivial at all: *Which does Judaism care more about — what animals you eat or how you earn your money?*

Answer: How you earn your money. As Meir Tamari, an Israeli economist, has noted, more than 100 commandments in the Torah address economics, but only 24 form the basis of traditional Jewish dietary practice.

Take Religious Values to Your Office

Rabbi Abraham Joshua Heschel once taught a class to rabbinical students at The Jewish Theological Seminary about a subject that most of them had probably never considered: Business ethics in Jewish law.

Heschel told them, "You have become skilled at spotting

blood in an egg. When there is blood in an egg, it becomes unkosher and unsuitable for eating. I hope you will be just as able to spot blood in money as well."

Heschel was saying that keeping kosher was very important, but that God cares about other things besides "religion." Judaism is about *profits* as well as *prophets*. Psalm 116:9 states, "I shall walk before God in the land of the living. The Talmud teaches that the "land of the living" is the market place. That is where life *happens* (Talmud, *Yoma* 71a). The sages of the Talmud said: "Whoever wants to be saintly should live according to the tractates of the Talmud dealing with commerce and finance" (Talmud, *Baba Kama* 30a).

Consider Ludwig Jesselson, the longtime chairman and C.E.O. of Phillip Brothers, a Manhattan-based international commodity trading company. When he died in 1993, he left a legacy of success — and of public service. He was a *baal tzedakah*, a master of righteous giving. By all accounts, he was a premier Jewish philanthropist of the 20th century.

In his eulogy for his father, Jesselson's son Michael said, "My father was the model that success can come without being at the expense of one's values. My father didn't have different lives — a business life, a private life, business friends, private friends. In business, I never heard my father make the excuse, 'Well, that's business.' He conducted himself the same way whether he was involved in business, social or communal activities. He acted with honesty, directness and an unfaltering respect for people regardless of age, intelligence, social position or religious beliefs."

People who so explicitly take their religious values to the office may be in the minority. According to Robert Wuthnow, professor of the sociology of religion at Princeton University, "Many people of faith leave their faith at the church door on Sunday, and on Monday behave just like everyone else." In a survey of over 2,000 workers, 40 percent reported arriving late to work during the previous month and more than 25 percent had used office equipment for personal purposes, covered up others' mistakes, bent the rules and bent the truth. Twenty percent reported not questioning things they suspected were unethical. Fourteen percent said that they had taken unauthorized time off. Three percent admitted to charging their employer for dubious expenses.

But the survey also discovered that *religion* is the single greatest factor in creating a more moral workplace. The more often people go to church, the less likely they are to deal unethically in business. Those who attend services weekly reported ethically questionable acts that were up to seven percentage points *less* than the average. And those who seldom or never attended services reported unethical behavior that was, on the average, seven points *higher* than the average.

Apparently the words of an anonymous Baptist preacher are true: "A religion that ain't good on Monday ain't good on Sunday."

God Cares about More Than Religion

Judaism also profoundly believes that religion has a message that goes beyond ritual. As Rabbi Alan Mittleman, a religion professor at Muhlenberg College, wrote, "A renewal of Jewish life requires a fresh consideration of the connections between religion and public affairs. Judaism is a religion of the classroom, but it is also a religion of marketplaces, courts, and operating rooms." This is what being a "light to the nations" is about.

American Jews live with a paradox. They are disproportionately represented on the "Fortune 500," run top universities, head major corporations and have scaled many of the walls of social exclusion that had formerly barred them. They are in the House and the Senate and the highest echelons of political power. They are a vital voice in the making of national and international policy.

The Jewish community has never been as powerful as it is now. Yet, this power often does not extend to its own community. True, the Orthodox world still has a sense of *"kashrut"* in business, but lacks the power to enforce sanctions beyond a small group. Non-Orthodox Jews, while embarrassed by those who are unscrupulous, usually do not exercise religious or communal sanctions against them. The liberal Jewish community is simply not put together that way. One wonders: Had there been such internal controls and sanctions, would they have discouraged the tragic spectacle of inside traders like Ivan Boesky, fraudulent nursing home operators, money launderers, and other stains on the image of the Jewish people?

But historically, Judaism was different. In the past, Jews set religious, moral, and economic standards for themselves —

and made sure they were obeyed. When in the third to sixth centuries of the Common Era, the rabbis of the Talmud spoke about business ethics, their words were not lofty speculation. In Babylonia, secular rulers authorized rabbis to regulate markets and judge business disputes. In the Middle Ages, Jewish law served as the civil law within the Jewish communal structure. Ever since the Enlightenment, when Jews entered the modern world and became subject to the laws of the state, Jews have lost *both* religious coercion and a sense of communal responsibility. With these have also gone communal sanction. This phenomenon is part of the mixed blessing of living in modern times.

The Basic Principles of Jewish Business Ethics

How can we hear again the Jewish voice in business? And what moral tone should it offer the business world?

To have a moral life, we must be self-critical.

It's too easy to be too easy on ourselves. As the Reform Jewish theologian Rabbi Eugene Borowitz has said: "We will have no significantly effective business ethics until we once again learn to feel shame for our business immoralities." Borowitz noted that we are neither so insensitive nor callous that we do not feel shame. We feel it when bungling a business deal or losing our clout or standing among our colleagues. But we need to feel it when making unethical business decisions, too.

"On the whole," he said, "we are not that invested in Judeo-

Christian ethics. Brazenness, rather than moral sensitivity, is often trumpeted as the sign of a competent executive."

The rabbis called this attitude *azut panim,* literally, "the strength of face," summoning the inner strength to face down every twinge of conscience. The sages said that this ability to dull the conscience ultimately caused the destruction of the Second Temple in Jerusalem in the year 70 C.E.

The inability to feel appropriate guilt over transgression sent the Jewish people into exile. Each of us needs to come home from our individual moral exiles.

We are bound together in a moral community.

A few months ago, a congregant told me, "The basis of all religion is probably the commandment 'Love your neighbor as yourself.' But industry is the opposite. It's 'Get them before they get you.' You have to get what you can out of people."

This rapacious world view unintentionally mimics the writings of the philosopher Thomas Hobbes, who believed that *homo hominis lupis:* "Each man is the other man's wolf." This may be the world in which many of us think we live, but it is not the world in which most of us *want* to live.

Judaism rejects that view. It prefers something more elegant: That we are made in God's image. We reject the words that were written over the gates of Buchenwald: *Jedem das seine,* "Every man for himself" — and we ask the rest of the world to do the same. We prefer to believe that we are part of a moral community that extends beyond us.

We are higher than animals —
and only a little lower than the angels.

People repeatedly say: "You can talk about spiritual and ethical values in business all you want. But if you bring those values to your business, you'll be at a disadvantage. There are predators out there."

Indeed, there are. But Jews reject the core belief of social Darwinism that only the strong survive. In Leviticus 11:13, we find the commandment not to eat vultures. Since few people actually have vulture on their menus, we interpret the verse metaphorically. If we are what we eat, it means that we should not become birds of prey.

People are more than what they can produce.

Martin Buber knew that we live in two realms: The realm of *I-thou,* in which God is implicated in the human relationship; and the realm of *I-it,* in which we use, categorize and objectify. Buber wanted us to reject the *I-itification* of the worker, the terrifying possibility that people will only become cogs in the machinery of their working lives.

In the words of the prominent Orthodox rabbi Marc Angel, "The teachings of Torah are different from the Torah of technology and the workplace. The Torah cares first about the well-being of people. Technology for its own sake can be demonic. Its sole value is in improving people's lives. It should be introduced with as much sensitivity as possible so that the fewest people are hurt. Those who are displaced should never have to feel that they are redundant. The value of a person's life is never measured by how valuable they are economically. Our goal is not how well we compete, but how well we provide for all the needs of people. Modern society asks: How much? Jewish tradition asks: Why?"

God is implicated in what we do.

There is a name for Jews' outrage about other Jews who are involved in unscrupulous business practices: *Hillul ha-shem.* To be unscrupulous is to desecrate God's Name, and by implication, to desecrate Judaism itself. The Talmud puts it quite clearly: Jews who profane the Name of God through their actions force non-Jews to say *Ain Torah l'Yisrael,* "The Jews don't have a Torah."

An Orthodox computer consultant once told me, "When I do business, I do business as a Jew. People know I'm Jewish; after all, I wear a *yarmulke* in the office. I follow a number of ethical rules in my work. Among them is not gossiping about people or clients or competitors. People know that this is a solid rule. I don't always succeed, but I believe that every encounter that I have with a client is an encounter that implicates the entire Jewish people, and I make sure that the way I behave is a *kiddush ha-shem,* a sanctification of the Name of God."

That also means that we must be particularly diligent when our business involves Jewish ritual. The Talmud gives us examples in which Jewish ritual encountered the profit motive. Rav, one of the two most important Babylonian Jewish authorities, said: "Earthenware pots in which leaven is cooked, and which absorbed and retained some of it, must be broken on Passover." This led some pot merchants to see an excellent business opportunity: People would have to shatter their leavened pots, and then they would have to pay unreasonable prices for new ones.

Samuel, Rav's colleague, dealt with this early case of the ethics of supply and demand by telling those merchants, "Unless you charge a fair price for your pots, I shall decide in accordance with Rabbi Simeon who *permits* the use of earthenware pots after Passover. Then people will not break their pots before Passover, as Rav suggested, and you will find yourselves abundantly overstocked."

The result of this tongue-lashing was a buyers' market on the pot exchange that year and for years to come.

What we do and how we do it survives us.

Although Jews do not fantasize much about what happens in the next world, one of the best exceptions to this rule are these words of the sage, Rava, from the Babylonian Talmud (*Shabbat* 31a): "When a person ascends to the ultimate judgement, they ask these questions: 'Did you set aside fixed time for study? Did you engage in the *mitzvah* of procreation? Did you hope for salvation?'"

But taking precedence over *those* questions is *this* one: "*Natata v'nasata be-emunah?* Did you conduct your business with faithfulness to the Jewish ethical tradition?"

We live in the world of flesh-and-blood, not the world of angels.

Judaism has always lived in "the real world." Therefore, a Jewish approach to business ethics must be realistic. Judaism has never fled from honest business competition. It has never believed that money is vulgar or that business is defiling. Nor is it opposed to wealth and prosperity. The most frequent euphemism in the Bible for success says that God was *with* someone, as in "God was with Joseph" in Egypt as he helped his master, Potiphar, prosper. It is not that we must choose *either* profits and riches *or* altruism and ethical responsibility. Judaism believes that one can — and should — have *both.* While *tzedakah* (righteous giving) is a *mitzvah*, poverty is not a virtue.

There is an interesting debate in the Talmud about the nature of competition in business. The premise is that a shopkeeper must not give free roasted nuts and corn to children whose mothers have sent them to shop because this encourages them to come only to him, and thus creates unfair competition. Yet other sages permitted this practice "because this shopkeeper can say to his competitors, 'I give them nuts, you give them plums!'" In other words, let the competitive chips fall where they may. In the same passage, it states that selling below the market price is permissible because it helps keep prices down.

Not Only What We Do, but How We Do It

The ultimate bottom line in business ethics is even if *what* we do is not very spiritual, *how* we do it can be. As the traditional blessing after meals states: "O Merciful One, may we earn our livelihood in a proper and not an improper way, with honor and not with shame." Even if our work itself does not allow us to reach the stars, at the very least we can and should deal ethically with people. When people carp that "It's a jungle out there," our job can be to sound a clarion call for sanity in the midst of that jungle.

"In a place where there are no people of decency," says *Pirke Avot,* the section of the Mishnah that deals with ethics, "strive to be a decent person."

This is the least — the very least — that we can do.

Making It Real in Your Life

- ***When have you been faced with difficult ethical decisions in your work? How did you deal with them?***
- ***Have you ever seen a colleague behave unethically? What did you do about it?***
- ***Do you ever reflect on your personal business ethics? What constitutes your code of business or professional ethics? How does it relate to what Judaism teaches?***
- ***What have you learned from Judaism about ethics? What do you wish you could have learned?***
- ***What can you do in your work to make Jewish ethical teachings come alive?***

Six

The Ultimate Business School Final Examination: *Leviticus 19*

"To test the worth of a man's religion, do business with him."

— *Bishop John Lancaster Spaulding, American church leader*

Say the word "holy" and most people think of vaulted ceilings in churches, silent prayer and monks chanting in a monastery. "Holy," we think, means untouchable. Chances are the word is said in hushed, reverential tones.

We assume that "holy" is not a word for this world. Or is it? "Holy" (in Hebrew, *kadosh*) is one of the central words in Judaism's spiritual vocabulary. When Jews affirm the holiness of Shabbat and thank God for wine, they say *kiddush.* In Jewish liturgy, the prayer that invokes Isaiah's vision of the celestials praising God ("Holy, holy, holy is the Lord of Hosts!") is the *kedusha.* When Jews get married, and thus create a holy relationship, the marriage ceremony is called *kiddushin.* When they encounter holiness by recalling someone who has died, they recite *Kaddish.* When they visit Jerusalem, they go to *ir ha-kodesh,* the holy city, located in a place that many call "the Holy Land," where Jews speak Hebrew, *lashon ha-kodesh,* the holy language. Jews, in fact, can't walk very far without encountering the term *kadosh* or its derivatives.

But note: Blessing wine or getting married or going to Jerusalem or singing God's praises doesn't make you holy. These things do, however, bring you into contact with holiness since holiness is an attitude towards life. Holiness means to venerate the divine, to sense the mystery and the knowledge that one has encountered God's reality; to possess an inkling that some realms are set-apart, unique, God-filled, that they are links between heaven and earth and manifestations of a shared reality with God. As Rabbi Lawrence Kushner said in *Honey From The Rock* (Jewish Lights), "There are worlds more real than this one. Shabbat is more real than Wednesday. Jerusalem is more real than Chicago. The *sukkah* [the booth used on the festival of Sukkot] is more real than a garage. *Tzedakah* [righteous giving] is more real than income tax." The basic premise of all religious life is that holy things are more *real,* more meaningful, more lasting than profane, ordinary, untouched-by-God things. The corollary of this supposition is that all things, potentially, can become holy.

In the Talmud, a rabbi audaciously remarked, "If I had been present at the revelation at Mount Sinai, I would have asked God for two tongues: One to speak the words of the world, and one to speak words of God." Holiness means to enter into a whole new conversation about the meaning of life; to ask yourself a whole new level of questions than those that the secular world usually poses; to speak the language of *what ought to be,* even when it means speaking against the language of the *what really is.* It means beginning to speak the words of God.

For example, these are *secular* questions: "What are my rights?" "How can I own it?" "What does the world owe me?" "Does it work?" "Will people approve of me?"

And these are *holy* questions: "What are my obligations?" "How can I proclaim in my deeds that God ultimately owns everything?" "What do I owe the world?" "Is this particular behavior *right*?" "Will God approve of me?"

That is why "holiness" is not divorced from this world. It is that which is very much *within* this world. In fact, when Jews try to come up with a term for "ethics," it usually comes out as "holy": Trying to be holy "like God is holy" (Lev. 19:1) — setting certain things, times, places and relationships aside for God, and bringing God into the world.

These are nice ideals. But how do we make them real?

Routes to Holiness

To find a detailed list of instructions on how to be holy, turn to Leviticus 19, the Holiness Code. This is the Torah's most systematic understanding of ethical behavior. It is so crucial to the way we live our lives that Reform congregations read it on Yom Kippur afternoon. Though Leviticus is often characterized as the manual of the ancient Jewish priests, Leviticus 19 is not just for those officiants at God's altar in the ancient Temple. It is addressed to the entire Jewish people, and by extension, to the entire world. It is not about the Biblical sacrificial system: Altars and blood and smoke and offerings. It is about "the real world" — and how to make it into a holier place.

Jews read sacred texts through the eyes of a commentator, ancient or modern. This is not to say that Jews cannot have their own opinions about the meaning of the text. They *can* — and they *should.* But traditional Torah study — and all of Judaism — begins with knowing how traditional commentators derived meaning from the words of the text. Their way of understanding becomes a gateway to our understanding. Such engagement with the past is the Jewish way of "standing on the shoulders of giants."

The most famous classic commentator was Rabbi Solomon ben Isaac (1040–1105). Known as Rashi, he was born in Troyes, France. Like all the great medieval teachers of Judaism, Rashi lived with his feet planted squarely in two worlds: The world of sacred endeavor and the world of work. Rashi lived in the city of Champagne, a major mercantile center. He knew about currency, banking and trade, soldering, engraving, weaving, agriculture and animal husbandry. He was also a wine merchant. In his "spare time," Rashi created the most important of all classic commentaries on the Hebrew Bible and the Talmud. Four centuries before the Renaissance, Rashi was a Renaissance man.

Rashi's commentary on the Torah is Jewish commentary *par excellence.* It greatly influenced Christian understandings of Scripture, and in traditional Jewish circles, one can't properly comprehend the Torah without understanding how Rashi understood the Torah. His commentary became such a benchmark because he masterfully presented his students with a digest of early rabbinic law and teaching that had been written at least six centuries before his time. This is ironic and telling. Rashi is the most respected of all Torah commentators precisely because he was so "unoriginal." He knew that he was simply a link in a chain, a bearer and a communicator of a sacred tradition.

Rashi was such a prominent commentator that his very name now means *any* commentary on a sacred text. I offer the following business ethics "Rashi" on certain verses of Leviticus 19 in the hope that it might become your way to find some holiness in the real world — just as Rashi found it in his.

> 1) God spoke to Moses, saying: 2) Speak to the whole Israelite community and say to them: You shall be holy, for I, the Eternal your God, am holy. 3) You shall each revere his mother and his father, and keep My sabbaths: I the Lord am your God. 4) Do not turn to idols or make molten gods for yourselves: I the Lord am your God....
>
> 9) When you reap the harvest of your land, you shall not reap all the way to the edges of your field, or gather the gleanings of your harvest. 10) You shall not pick your vineyard bare, or gather the fallen fruit of your vineyard; you shall leave them for the poor and the stranger: I the Eternal am your God. 11) You shall not steal; you shall not deal deceitfully in My name, profaning the name of your God: I am the Eternal. 13) You shall not defraud your neighbor. You shall not commit robbery. The wages of a laborer shall not remain with you until morning.

14) You shall not insult the deaf, or place a stumbling block before the blind. You shall fear your God: I am the Eternal. 15) You shall not render an unfair decision: do not favor the poor or show deference to the rich; judge your neighbor fairly. 16) Do not deal basely with your fellows. Do not profit by the blood of your neighbor. I am the Eternal....

35) You shall not falsify measures of length, weight, or capacity. 36) You shall have an honest balance, honest weights, an honest *ephah,* and an honest *hin.* I the Eternal am your God who freed you from the land of Egypt. 37) You shall faithfully observe all My laws and all My rules: I am the Eternal.

"Do not turn to idols....": Verse 4

Knowing that there is a God in the world is the first step in being ethical in business. "I have set the Eternal before me at all times," wrote the Psalmist. *At all times* — even, and especially, in one's business.

In Tom Wolfe's novel *The Bonfire of the Vanities,* Sherman McCoy, the tragic bond trader, describes himself as a Master of the Universe. Sherman McCoy hungered more for power than for money. He had a grandiose, self-destructive fantasy of omnipotence, one in which the rules of ordinary mortals did not apply to him.

"Master of the Universe" is a literal translation of one of God's names: *Ribono shel olam,* the Ultimate Master of the Universe. That was Sherman McCoy's problem: He wanted to be God. But there isn't room in this universe for more than one Ultimate Master.

Indeed, that is the hidden code of Jewish business ethics: God is in charge. God's sovereignty extends over every aspect of our lives, including our economic life. God ultimately owns everything. This means that we cannot hoard wealth that we do not, ultimately, own. We are merely borrowing it.

"When you reap the harvest of your land...": Verse 9

In his book *Capitalism and Freedom,* economist Milton Friedman states: "There is one and only one social responsibility of business: To use its resources and engage in activities designed to increase its profits so long as it stays within the rules of the game, which is to say, engages in open and free competition without deception or fraud." Friedman believes that corporations should not be compelled to use their profits for charitable purposes or to aid society.

But Milton Friedman is wrong, and the Torah is right.

The above Torah verse teaches us about two *mitzvot.* The first is *peah:* Leaving the corners of the field uncut so that the poor can help themselves to what was left behind. The very minimum that Jewish tradition says that we must leave behind is one-60th of the yield. The Mishnah, the post-Biblical code of Jewish law, says that the reward for this *mitzvah* comes *not* in this world, but in the world to come.

The second *mitzvah* is *leket:* The reaper lets grain stalks fall to the ground so the poor can find them. Together, these two comprise basic *tzedakah* (righteous giving).

Thank God — literally, *thank God* — that there are business people who apply these commandments to their work. Fred

Schwartz, who, as "Fred the Furrier," revolutionized the retailing of furs in the United States, once told me his philosophy of business: "The responsibility that I have towards the continuity of society underpins all that I do. Frankly, the idea of doing *mitzvot* in my work make me bristle. I don't see it as a separate part of business. It is woven into the fabric of my life. If you see it as separate, it becomes a noble, gratuitous deed on your part, as opposed to an inherent obligation."

"I always knew that I would gravitate to *tzedakah,*" he said. "I am involved with close to 30 charities. Most are concerned with improving the quality of life or education in New York City. Yes, you can be aggressive and acquisitive in business, but there is also the requirement to *maintain* the world, which Jews call *tikkun olam.* There are many values more important than money. I believe in giving, but not only money. You have to give of yourself as well."

There are numerous models in the business world of people who have made community service a model. (There is even a magazine that covers this field, *Business Ethics*). Consider just one example: The company that makes my favorite ice cream, Ben and Jerry's, the Waterbury, Vermont based ice cream company, founded in 1978 by best friends Ben Cohen and Jerry Greenfield. It is the second largest purveyor of superpremium ice cream in the country.

A few years ago, Ben Cohen said: "Money is the most powerful force in our society and business in America is incredibly powerful. The question is how to harness the power of business to improve the quality of life." Ben and Jerry believe in changing the direction of a company's bottom line. They believe, in fact, that there are *two* bottom lines: How much money (or profits) are left over at the end of the year, and how much the company has contributed to the quality of life. They have said: "Giving away a portion of our profits [read: *leaving corners of the field]* is nice, but it is a minor thing compared to the positive social impact we can have by making the way we run our business every day a reflection of our conscious caring for the people around us."

Ben and Jerry's packages are advertisements for their social message. The small type on a pint of Rainforest Crunch made a pitch for preserving the Brazilian rainforest. The wrapper on a Peace Pop advocated using one percent of the Pentagon's budget to promote peace. New York Super Fudge Chunk announces that Ben and Jerry's supports family farms by buying milk and cream from the St. Albans Cooperative Creamery, which is owned by 500 Vermont family farmers. The lids of various flavors proclaim that "1 out of 4 kids in the U.S. is born into poverty. Together we can change that. Call 1-800-BJ-KIDS-1." Thirty-five cents from the sale of every pint of factory seconds go to local causes chosen by the store owner who has sold that pint. Seven and one-half percent of Ben and Jerry's pre-tax profits go to the Ben and Jerry's Foundation, which funds such projects as AIDS research and helping the homeless.

What Ben and Jerry's does *matters.* It matters to their workers. A visitor to one of their factory ice cream booths cannot help but be taken by the buoyant faces of the employees, conveying that these are people with a *mission*. They believe that they are making a better world through better ice cream. And that belief has created a working atmosphere of *joy* and commitment. Ben and Jerry's entrepreneurial experiment is such a success that I'm convinced that ice cream just might be part of the process of bringing us all just a bit closer to the Messianic Age.

Thankfully, Ben and Jerry are not alone in their interpretation of what it means to do well in the business world. An Orthodox architect once told me, "By following the ethical values inherent in Judaism, I do an honest day's work. I charge reasonable fees, I give *tzedakah* [money and free services], and I refuse to accept illegal work. The reward for being ethical is a reward in itself because I sleep well at nights. But the bottom line is that I have a creative ability that almost comes naturally to me. I thank God each night for this ability that was bestowed upon me and for strengths that reflect what God wants me to do."

"There is another reason," he continued, "why I occasionally do *pro bono* work if it will better our society. Lately, I have devoted my entire practice to designing buildings that are environmentally sensitive and energy efficient. I use only natural materials, avoid those that are toxic and install solar heating and cooling systems and water and waste recycling systems. I also try to bring back to neighborhoods the quality of life that's missing in most suburban sprawl areas."

Ben and Jerry's and other companies involved in *tzedakah* are leaving "corners of the field." They are letting whatever falls from their hands go into someone else's hands. They are doing holy work.

"You shall not steal": Verse 11

This means not only stealing goods, but also the sin of misrepresentation. In Hebrew, it is called *genevat daat,* literally, "stealing someone's mind."

It means not engaging in "bait-and-switch" tricks that are consumers' nightmares. It means not dressing up a product so that it looks better than it is, especially since the *Shulchan Aruch,* the classic 16th century code of Jewish law, teaches that "one is forbidden to beautify the article being sold in order to create a false impression. It is [also] forbidden to dye a slave's hair or beard in order to make him appear young....One is not allowed to paint old baskets to make them appear new nor is one allowed to soak meat in water to make it white and look fat" (Shulchan Aruch, *Hoshen Mishpat, Hilchot Genevah,* section 358).

This is not only true of *products,* but also of *people.* How do we handle references for employees who may not have done a great job, but who we want to succeed anyway because we like them? Do we bend the truth to help them? How do we handle references for *current* employees whom we like and want to keep? Do we bend the truth about them *negatively* so we can help *ourselves* out? How do we present ourselves in job interviews? Do we say what we think the potential employer wants to hear? Or are we honest with them and with ourselves? When we are in unpleasant (and ethically compromising) situations at work, do we speak our mind? Or do we misrepresent ourselves, our ethics and our values?

Not defrauding, robbing, or withholding your laborer's wages: Verse 13

The Hebrew term for oppressing workers, *oshek,* means "taking advantage of a worker." The Bible generally assumed that workers were relatively powerless and easily intimidated.

Oshek means not paying people what they deserve or not paying the going rate for a particular job or not paying someone on time. The Torah teaches, "You shall not abuse a needy and destitute laborer, whether a fellow countryman or a stranger in one of the communities of your land. You must pay him his wages on the same day, before the sun sets..." (Deut. 24:15).

So much for "the check being in the mail." People are made in God's Image. Therefore, we can't let them barter their dignity by pleading for what is due them.

To the traditional definition of *oshek* can be added a new one: Sexual harassment, which lets the relatively powerful take advantage of the relatively powerless.

Being made in God's Image means that if people are humiliated, God is humiliated, too.

Not putting a stumbling block before the blind: Verse 14

Few people are malicious enough to *literally* put a hazardous obstacle in front of a blind person so that the handicapped person falls over. Jewish tradition understands this prohibition as meaning that we should not tempt another person by preying on his or her weakness or "blindness." It means not misleading people. Deuteronomy 27:18 more clearly fleshes out the meaning of this *mitzvah:* "Cursed be he who misdirects a blind person on his way."

What are the practical implications of this commandment?

- Not giving someone unwise business advice. Rashi interpreted the verse this way: "Do not say to someone, 'Sell your field and buy a donkey,' when the whole purpose of the transaction is to obtain possession of that same field."
- Financial advisors and brokers not giving advice that is in *their* best financial interests. Or, to move this *mitzvah* into the realm of the truly saintly, it means not selling something that the purchaser can clearly not afford.
- Advertisers must be morally scrupulous. Advertising, for instance, that "sells" the idea that smoking is glamorous does a disservice to young people who are "blinded" by imagined status. Liquor commercials on television shows aimed at young people only encourage teenaged alcohol use.

"Not putting a stumbling block before the blind" means not deluding those whom our popular culture has dazzled into believing that they want or need certain things. Many parents agree that the cacophony of Saturday morning toy and candy commercials aimed at youngsters falls into this moral category.

"Not putting a stumbling block before the blind" means not to use glamorous, waif-like women to sell certain products. This sends a destructive message to women that only "thin" is beautiful.

"Do not profit by the blood of your neighbor": Verse 16

It is forbidden to pursue a livelihood in a way that would endanger another or gain profit at another person's expense.

This means rejecting business opportunities that contribute to pollution of the environment. As managing editor Craig Cox wrote in *Business Ethics* magazine, this means "ignoring the siren song of cheap labor, lax government regulations, and instant profitability echoing from beyond our borders."

It also means being sensitive about "downsizing" in a time of merger mania and the diminishing of white-collar jobs — "getting lean without getting mean."

And it means not selling people things that are morally or physically harmful, such as cigarettes, drugs, pornography or weapons. Jewish law would reject the quip of Sylvia Daniel, the Tennessee woman known as "Machine Gun Mama," who manufactures machine guns and who says, "It may be immoral, but the bottom line is money." Jewish law supports various forms of gun control, mostly because it can't figure out why someone would even want a gun. It also frowns on hunting as sport because it violates *tzaar baalei chayim,* the prohibition against violence to animals. Maimonides even prohibited Jews from being weapons dealers because they would inadvertently help their enemies procure weapons that could be the source of their own victimization.

Have honest measures: Verses 35–36

Deut. 25:13-16 further fleshes out the meaning of this verse: "You shall not have in your pouch alternate weights, a larger and a smaller. You must have completely honest weights and completely honest measures if you are to endure long on the soil that the Eternal your God is giving you. For everyone who does those things, everyone who deals dishonestly, is abhorrent to the Eternal your God."

Abhorrent. The Hebrew word is *toevah,* literally, "abomination." The same word describes the Torah's opinion on child sacrifice and bestiality. To say the least, it is a strong moral judgement. Likewise, Jewish tradition notices that it is difficult to atone for using improper weights and measures, because of the impossibility of remembering everyone who bought a product that was weighed on these scales.

Consider the verses in Deuteronomy 25 that immediately follow the discussion about improper weights and measures. They tell the story of the ancient Amalek, the desert raiders who attacked the Jewish people as they were going out of Egypt. Some rabbis say that the Torah places the two passages adjacent to each other so that we will know that the punishment for improper business dealings is our potential destruction. *Spiritual* and *ethical* corruption leads to *physical* perdition.

Where does all this finally bring us?

Judaism Teaches Us to Say "Yes" — *and* "No"

First, remember that virtually each commandment ends with the refrain: "I am the Eternal." Our ethics, therefore, are not free-wheeling or autonomous. It is not enough to refrain from the bad or pursue the good because "it makes sense to do so" or "it's company policy" or "it will help my corporate image" or "it's a federal guideline." As the Jewish theologian Will Herberg said, "Hebraic religion says *no* to society whenever society, in its pride, makes claims to absoluteness." Judaism knows all too well that societal norms are very mercurial and sometimes highly dangerous. In Nazi Germany, killing Jews was a "societal norm." In some African cultures, ritual mutilation of women is a "societal norm." Judaism — and Judaism's sense of God-centered ethics — directs us away from the relativism that is too prevalent in our society and in the world at large.

Some societal norms steer us toward conspicuous consumption, greed and a lack of social conscience. The religious voice in society is the one that stands up and says: "Wait a minute. This is not what God intended when we were instructed to create a civilization."

Second, we ultimately find ourselves going back to the beginning of the chapter. *Kedoshim tihiyu,* "You shall be holy."

We become holy when we strive to become like God. We become holy when we try to raise ourselves above the level of the animals, when we aspire to a life that is set apart from the mundane, when we pay attention to the ethical implications of what we do.

Ben Cohen addressed this very idea in a Ben and Jerry's annual report a few years ago: "Corporations which exist solely to maximize profit become disconnected from their soul — the spiritual interconnectedness of humanity. Like individuals, businesses can conduct themselves with the knowledge that the hearts, souls, and spirits of all people are interconnected, so that as we help others we cannot help helping ourselves. It makes no sense to compartmentalize our lives — to be cut-throat in business and then volunteer some time or donate some money to charity....If business is the most powerful force in the world, it stands to reason that business sets the tone for our society."

Sometimes I believe that it is not true that each of us is *a* self. Rather, we are an entire committee of selves. But I am chastened by the notion that religious people, of any faith, have a unique task: To find the place within where all those selves come together: Father, mother, sister, brother, son, daughter, friend, neighbor, business person, and the person of faith. It is called the search for integrity.

Rav Ben Zion Uziel, the late Sephardic Chief Rabbi of Israel, put it in a way that lets us hear the echoes of 2,000 years of ethical striving. "Labor is an intellectual and ethical sanctuary which elevates the soul, improves the spirit, and makes workers into people of kindness, compassion, love, affection for all creations, open-hearted to all that are created in the image of God."

Imagine your own life that way, as a sanctuary, as having a

Holy Ark within it: A place where *your* Torah is kept, the Torah that you are writing even now with your life. Over that inner Ark is inscribed the words that most commonly adorn arks in synagogues around the world. "Know before Whom you stand." In all that we do, we can strive to stand before God.

Standing before God will implant within you happiness and fulfillment. Some of the happiest people I know have made *shalom* with all the pieces that comprise their lives: Their personal lives, their business lives, their religious lives. Making *shalom*, peace, within yourself allows you to be one, just as God is one.

This is called *integrity*. In Yiddish, it's also called *menschlicheit* (upward striving and decency).

Ultimately, it's what it means to get closer to God — and to stand in God's Presence.

Making It Real in Your Life

- ***When have you experienced issues such as those described in this chapter?***
- ***Do you think it is possible to live a religious life centered around ethics and morality in the business world?***
- ***When has your integrity been challenged by your work? How did you resolve this?***
- ***How can you set out a strategy to make the teachings of this chapter come alive in your own workplace?***

Seven

Shattering the Idols of the Workplace

"The gods we worship write their names on our faces, be sure of that. And we will worship something — have no doubt of that either. We may think that our tribute is paid in secret in the dark recesses of the heart — but it will out. That which dominates our imagination and our thoughts will determine our life and character. Therefore it behooves us to be careful what we are worshipping, for what we are worshipping, we are becoming."

— *Gates of Prayer,* Reform movement's prayerbook

Each generation of children hears one of the most famous Jewish stories as if it was being told for the first time. It is a midrash, a legend that imagines the childhood of Abraham, the first Jew.

Abraham's father, Terach, is in the idol business in Ur, a city in ancient Sumer. He goes away on business, and leaves his young son, Abram, in charge of the idol shop. Abram, who is later called Abraham, shatters all the idols in the store with a stick, then places the stick in the hand of the largest idol. When Terach gets back, he sees the ruined merchandise.

"What happened?" he demands.

"Oh, father, it was terrible," says Abram. "The small idols got hungry and started fighting for food. Then, the large idol got angry and broke the smaller ones into little pieces. It was frightening. I don't want to talk about it."

"Wait a second," says Terach. "Idols don't get hungry. They don't get angry. They don't speak. They're just...they're just clay idols."

"So," Abram asks with a smile, "why do you worship them?"

Let's All Be Idol-Breakers

This midrash is an essential part of the collective memory of the Jewish people. It tells them that they are the children of an iconoclast, a contrarian, an idol-smasher. Abraham's shattering of the idols initiated not only the first formative stages of the Jewish people, but of all Western religion.

But idolatry is deeper and profoundly more enervating than worshipping gods made of stone and wood. Idolatry distorts values. It elevates to ultimate importance and awesome holiness something that is not ultimately important and holy. It can corrupt us and lead us astray, and fill us with false, vapid hopes and aspirations.

The legend of Abraham's shattering of the idols is so powerful that when Paul Tillich, the modern Protestant thinker, first heard the tale, he remarked that contemporary society had become the equivalent of Terach's idol boutique. By our worshipping the ephemeral, the trivial, even those things that are good and beautiful, but not ultimate, we become idolaters.

Every society has its equivalent of the idol shop that Abram's father owned. In contemporary America, some of the most persistent most common idols are the twin gods of workaholism and careerism. The first consumes our time and our passions; the second falsely displaces all else that can satisfy us. Together, the two are the narcotics of modern America:

addicting and alluring, they are anything but truly, genuinely fulfilling.

Arise, Ye Prisoners of Your Labors: Work Can Be Slavery

On the gates of Auschwitz were written the infamous words *"Arbeit macht frei,"* "Work shall set you free." This was the grim lie of the Nazi work camps: Work would bring freedom to the worker. But Auschwitz was the antithesis of freedom. Its purpose was to confirm slavery and extract a death of the body and spirit from the worker.

In a sense, a small hidden spark of the mentality of Auschwitz lingers in our world. These are the fruits of that mentality: If we judge ourselves and judge others only by the goods or services that we produce, if we believe that to *be* more is to *do* more, then we are truly slaves to what we do. Work becomes an end in itself.

We eventually conclude that if we are *only* what we do, then to *be* "more," we must do more and produce more. This is no less than the demonic lie of Auschwitz. Instead of liberating us, work enslaves us and owns us.

The word for this is workaholism. As management consultant Diane Fassel wrote in *Working Ourselves to Death,* "Work is God for the compulsive worker, and nothing gets in the way of this God." Work becomes an end in itself, a way to escape from family, from the inner life, from the world. A psychologist friend of mine recently told me about a workaholic client who constantly brings work home. His wife and children resent the time that he spends away from them, and justifiably so, since he wonders if his compulsive work habits mask a fear of intimacy. At one point, the therapist told the client to log the number of hours he spent at work, and the number of hours at leisure. The client was shocked at the results. He now knows what he is doing, but like all addictions, it is very difficult to change.

According to Workaholics Anonymous, anyone who agrees with at least three of the following questions is either a workaholic or a potential workaholic:*

1. Do you get more excited about your work than about family or anything else?
2. Are there times when you can charge through your work and other times when you can't get anything done?
3. Do you take work with you to bed? On weekends? On vacation?
4. Is work the activity you like to do best and talk about most?
5. Do you work more than 40 hours a week?
6. Do you turn your hobbies into money-making ventures?
7. Do you take complete responsibility for the outcome of your work efforts?
8. Have your family or friends given up expecting you on time?
9. Do you take extra work because you are concerned

* Source: Workaholics Anonymous, P.O. Box 289, Menlo Park, CA 94026-0289. Used with permission.

that it won't otherwise get done?

10. Do you underestimate how long a project will take and then rush to complete it?
11. Do you believe that it is O.K. to work long hours if you love what you are doing?
12. Do you get impatient with people who have other priorities besides work?
13. Are you afraid that if you don't work hard you will lose your job or be a failure?
14. Is the future a constant worry for you even when things are going very well?
15. Do you do things energetically and competitively, including play?
16. Do you get irritated when people ask you to stop working so you can do something else?
17. Have your long hours hurt your family or other relationships?
18. Do you think about your work while driving, falling asleep or when others are talking?
19. Do you work or read during meals?
20. Do you believe that more money will solve the other problems in your life?

Workaholism is literally fatal. Its toxic fruits are heart disease, hypertension, gastric problems, depression, exhaustion, vague feelings of emptiness and detachment and a lack of meaning. But it is not unique to America. In Japan, *karoshi,* or "death from overwork," is the second largest killer of working males and accounts for 10 percent of Japan's death rate.

Like other addictions, workaholism consumes the addict's time, energy and thoughts. Yet, it is the only addiction in which the addict takes *pride.* A few months ago, I met with some friends over coffee. One worried that he was becoming a workaholic. He described a life of constant rushing; of non-stop busyness; of being unable to say "no" to the constant demands that he was placing upon himself. His life was a succession of lists, lists, lists. It was a life in which he could not take days off or find pleasure in small things.

Despite all this, his confession that he had become a workaholic was greeted with knowing laughter.

Why the chuckles? I realized later that if he had said he was an alcoholic, a sexaholic, a drug addict, there would have been sympathy and compassion. But instead, there was laughter. Workaholism is the only addiction that is socially acceptable because we think it is socially productive. It is also, we often think, *required* of us.

In Leo Tolstoy's short story "How Much Land Does A Man Need?", a Russian travels to the Bashkirs, a tribe in the hinterlands. They offer to give him as much land as he can cover on foot in one day. The man starts his frenetic journey. As the sun sets, he collapses in exhaustion and dies. The amount of land that he ultimately gets is a six-foot plot of earth as a final resting place. In our grasping for the material benefits of our society, we are not different from Tolstoy's character.

How much do we really need? How much do we have to work to get it? And what, in the end, satisfies and speaks to us?

The answers to these questions are complex and often elusive. They depend on each person's peculiar constellation of drive and ambition, on his or her desire to impress others or desire to impress themselves — and how that need can be met. But to so extensively believe that work alone can enrich and satisfy our lives is to place such hope in ephemera. For at the end of the day and the end of our lives, all we will have accomplished is to have spent years and years in our offices, and to ask the eternal question, "Is that all there is?"

A Career Can Become Tyranny

In his book *Remembering Denny,* Calvin Trillin wrote about the tragic story of his friend, Roger "Denny" Hansen, a "golden boy" from Southern California who went to Yale in the 1950s. Denny was "most likely to succeed" — at everything. *Life* magazine, which saw him as the paradigmatic American boy, even covered his college graduation. Denny lived with an "impostor complex." After he successfully met each challenge in life, he secretly thought that he'd "gotten away with it." Next time, the "real" Denny would catch up to him. Years later, amid deep conflicts over his life, Denny committed suicide.

Trillin's lament for his old friend is particularly moving:

"What is the criterion for promise fulfilled? A listing in *Who's Who?* A listing in *Forbes* magazine's annual issue devoted to the richest people in America? A seat in the Senate? A lifetime of service? A ticket that has been punched so many times that it's practically in tatters?"

Careerism is an orientation in which career is considered the primary, most important aim of life — and to which all else is sacrificed. To some degree, almost everyone is afflicted with it, since the concept of "career" has so ballooned that it is now often synonymous with one's identity. As the Hebrew/Yiddish writer, Reuben Brainin, observed, "As a man attaches himself to his work and dedicates his powers and talents to it, so it begins to be an aim and purpose in itself and brings contentment to him. At that point, one becomes subject, unwittingly, to its goals and obligations."

Such narrow, misfocused judgement starts innocently enough with a game that we play as children: "What are you going to do when you grow up?" But it eventually permeates everything we do: The party. The barbecue. Even that innocent-seeming introductory query, "So, what do you do?," which really means "What are you able to do?" All this transmutes into a chain of self-evaluating, self-deprecating thoughts: I am only what I do. I am only my profession, my career, my job, my paycheck, my possessions.

For Jews, the issue is even more pronounced, since their history has created a certain predisposition to careerism. In *Tribes: How Race, Religion and Identity Determine Success in the New Global Economy,* Joel Kotkin wrote that since the early Middle Ages, Jews always did best in the unexplored frontiers of trade. Because Jews were banned from certain occupations, they created their own niches in such emerging fields as diamonds, communications, fashion, retailing, entertainment, psychotherapy. Because of this, Jews always preferred the independence of self-employment. As the Talmud says: "Skin a carcass on the street rather than be dependent on other people."

In less than a century, American Jews have gone from Ellis Island to the fast track. This journey has devalued the traditional role of the parent as nurturer and teacher, while emphasizing almost exclusively the role of provider.

In a sense, this is not new. A Yiddish song, *"Mayn Yingele"* ("My Little One") is as poignant now as it was when written in 1897. In it, a father sings:

> "I have a son, a little son,
> A boy completely fine.
> When I see him it seems to me
> That all the world is mine.
> But seldom, seldom do I see
> My child awake and bright;
> I only see him when he sleeps;
> I'm only home at night.
> It's early when I leave for work;
> When I return it's late.
> Unknown to me is my own flesh,
> Unknown is my child's face.
> When I come home so wearily
> In the darkness after day,
> My pale wife exclaims to me:
> 'You should have seen our child play.'
> I stand beside his little bed,
> I look and try to hear.

In his dream he moves his lips:
'Why isn't Papa here?'

"Mayn Yingele" laments how working men's participation in their children's lives had shrunk. The father in the song probably worked in a sweat shop on New York's Lower East Side. He had no choice about how long or how hard he worked. His great-grandchildren may now have moved uptown or to the suburbs, out of the sweatshops and into the high-rise offices of midtown. Yet, the lament — and the parenting styles — are tragically similar. Our culture transmits a message that is simultaneously powerful and sad: To be "successful," one must be a high-powered professional who devotes day and night to a successful career.

No one — not men, women, or children — are immune from the effects of careerism. Writer Sharon Strassfeld, who is half of a dual-career couple, has lamented that she has "found myself arranging playdates [for her child] with housekeepers who were themselves bewildered by the array of after-school activities their young charges had been signed up for." Even though parents must accompany their children in the nursery her child attends three mornings a week, Strassfeld observes that "Parents who were willing to commit in that way were like dinosaurs: Extinct."

Amy Eilberg, the first woman rabbi in the Conservative movement, once observed that "feminism is not about abandonment of family. Feminism is about removing artificial barriers to women's fulfillment, about allowing women access to zealously guarded male spheres of activity. Feminism does not mean jettisoning all that has always been central to women's lives: love and care, nurturance and connectedness, family and relationship."

Rabbi Eilberg ultimately resigned from her rabbinic position so she could spend more time with her family. In her resignation letter to her congregation, she said, "My daughter's first sentence was 'Bye-bye, Ema-shul.' The words were too chilling to be cute or endearing." The reality was stark: For her daughter, Ema ("Mother" in Hebrew) was someone who was always leaving her to go to the "shul" (the synagogue) to work.

Careerism's second casualty is *leisure.* Ideally, leisure should mean blank, unstructured time, time for re-creation. Yet, this is exactly what terrifies many of us. Social critic Barbara Ehrenreich has observed that "busyness has become an important insignia of upper-middle class status. Eating is giving way to 'grazing' — the unconscious ingestion of unidentified foods while drafting a legal brief...."

Consumerism: A False God

All too often, when we are not consumed with *earning* money, we are consumed with *spending* it. The opening of a new mall is heralded and attended like the faithful once attended the opening of a new cathedral. Consumerism can replace leisure and almost become a punitive passion, as in the catch phrase, "Shop till you drop" — or the classic one-line meditation on mortality: "Whoever dies with the most toys, wins."

Fear of leisure is related to fear of retirement. I once discussed the concept of retirement with an older colleague, who chastised me, "Don't be *morbid.*" Morbid, as in "death-like." To not work is to not *be.* I often read obituaries in the newspaper. The wording of death notices is a mini-course about the essence of American civilization: They always list the *occupation* of the deceased first, and *relationships* last: "Irving Cohen, investment banker, dead at 86....He is survived by his wife, Sheila...." But, when Jews die, they are traditionally dressed in shrouds which have no pockets because we take nothing with us. Those we leave behind and who weep for us could generally care less about our curriculum vitae.

The third casualty of careerism is *the life of the spirit.*

The Psalmist cried, "It is time to work for God; they have nullified Your Torah!" Yet, modernity has left us little time to work for God, and by doing so, has nullified the sacred words of our tradition.

Ritual, festivals, sacred poetry, wine, spices, candles and song are poetic evocations. They are about dreams and visions, about landscapes not of our making, about stories and images, values and goals. They are a celebration of being. They are not utilitarian. They are not connected to career advancement, to enriching our bank accounts, to padding our resumes. Hence, those activities are often alien to us. And in our triage of time, they often go by the wayside.

But, sometimes something happens to bring us home.

How to Find Your Balance

Morris Smith used to spend 16 hours a day managing a massive $20 billion investment portfolio: The world's biggest mutual fund, Fidelity Investments' Magellan Fund. His only time out was Shabbat, which saved him from physical and psychological self-destruction. "Without Shabbat," he said, "I would have been a seven-day-a-week animal."

Each work day, Smith awoke at 5:40 a.m., was in shul by 6:05 a.m., on the train to Boston at 6:50, in the office at 7:30. His day included a brief break for dinner. But by 7:30 in the evening, he was back to the grindstone until 11:30. On Saturday nights after Shabbat ended, he would work until one in the morning.

Eventually, the thrill of finding the most profitable investments for billions of dollars began to wane. One day, while doing his Passover shopping in a supermarket, he began to make his escape plans, to create his own Haggadah of Exodus from an inner Pharaoh.

In April, 1992, Smith, then 34 years old, told Fidelity he was moving to Israel with his family. On one level, things haven't changed that much now that he lives in the north Jerusalem neighborhood of Ramot. He rises even earlier than he did in Boston. But now, after going to synagogue, he heads off to a yeshiva in Jerusalem's Old City to study Talmud. He's making plans to invest in various businesses, although he won't go near a mutual fund. Life is still hectic, but he has restored a sense of balance. He is living up to his resignation pronouncement: "There is more to life than money and management."

Morris Smith's decision to leave Fidelity took him from one translation of *avodah* to the other: From *work* to *worship*.

Few people can afford to do what Morris Smith did. Few people may even *want* to do it. After all, moving to Israel and studying in a *yeshiva* is not everyone's dream. But Morris Smith did find the place within himself that was holy, that was distinct from fantasies of career advancement and material riches: He decided to liberate himself from the fast track.

Many people make choices similar to Morris Smith. As Amy Saltzman wrote in *Downshifting: Reinventing Success on a Slower Track,* some decide to end or reverse their upward career climb — or to totally shift careers. In a recent survey of 1,000 men and women who are professionals, 82 percent of the women and 78 percent of the men said they would choose a career path with flexible full-time work hours and more family time, but slower career advancement. Two out of every three people surveyed said they were willing to reduce their work hours and salaries by an average of 13 percent so they could have more family time. Those numbers reflect Saltzman's suspicion that Americans are functioning "on remote control": Going through the motions, but forgetting the point.

But there *is* a point. To get to it we have to go from a life of external *coercion* to a life of internal *covenant.* We have to acknowledge a God who lives outside of us, but whose presence can nourish us from within.

And we have to shift the ultimate meaning of our lives from the demands that society has placed on us to the demands that we — and God — place on us; to have the courage to lift our eyes to what is beyond us and to sense what is most deeply within us. Only then can we court the realities that now elude us, and reap the truths that seem to so determinedly escape us.

Making It Real in Your Life

- ***Have you noticed any workaholic or careerist tendencies in yourself? How have you dealt with them?***
- ***What other "idols" are found in your workplace? How can you shatter them?***
- ***Do you ever feel that you are on "remote control"? How can you get control over your work-life and your career?***
- ***What one thing can you do today to free yourself? What one thing can you do tomorrow?***

Eight

Restoring Balance to Our Work Lives: *Specific Things You Can Do*

"Servants of time are slaves of slaves
The servant of God alone is free
When each one therefore seeks his lot
My soul says, 'God my lot shall be.'"
— Yehuda Halevi, medieval Spanish Jewish theologian and poet

In *The Music of Chance*, a novel by Paul Auster, two men lose everything they own in an all-night poker game with two eccentric lottery-winners. They are forced to pay up by constructing a wall on the estate of the millionaires. During their several months of work, they have several chances to escape. Not only do they fail to notice each one, but, truth be told, they gradually came to love the wall they build.

The story of these two men is too often our story. We frequently erect walls around our lives, walls that fence us in and constrain us. They blind us from the possibilities and the potentials both within us and around us. Sometimes, like the two laborers in Auster's *The Music of Chance*, we mistake the wall for the finer truths in life.

It is time to escape the confines of these walls, to escape from the inner slavery and the inner Pharaoh which we have allowed to enslave us. Below are eight gates of liberation from this bondage of the contemporary workplace.

I. Get a life

Many people in high-powered professions, as well as a decent number of those in lesser professions, seem to have no interests outside of work, nothing else to which to give themselves. As a letter writer in the journal *Sh'ma* observed about the private lives of Jewish public figures, "The competition at the very top of the heap is so intense that any distraction such as vacations, outside interests or taking time off for the Jewish holidays puts them at a disadvantage, or at least what they perceive to be one. The heart of the problem is that just those people who should be leaders of communities are too wrapped up in their work lives to have time for anything else. All too often, the brightest Jews are simply so over-committed in their own work that they don't have the time for synagogue, to say nothing of serious participation in Jewish organizational work."

The Midrash contains a tantalizing interpretation of the hidden meaning of the Priestly Benediction (Numbers 6): "May God bless you and keep you...." According to the Midrash, "May God bless you" means "to be blessed with wealth and possessions," and "May God keep you" means "May God keep your wealth and possessions from possessing *you*."

It is too easy to be possessed by our professions, by the status they confer or the material benefits they reap. To move beyond that, do something that is spiritually refreshing. Get involved in synagogue or church. Feed the homeless. Care for AIDS patients. Volunteer for a non-profit board. Do anything that offers you a sense of altruism and a connection to something higher. From his pulpit in Chicago, Reform Rabbi Joseph Edelheit once told his congregants how people waste time, then challenged them to sanctify their time by hugging cocaine-addicted babies in a local hospital.

"Not only did people take me up on the offer," he said later, "but they told me that it was the high point of the week." Find the places in your life in which people are not potential customers, colleagues or competitors. Determine how they — and you — can be compatriots in making the world more whole and a little bit closer to what God hoped for during Creation.

II. Discover Sabbath: More than candles, wine, and services

One of the eccentric millionaires in Auster's *The Music of Chance* built a scale model of the way he hoped the world would look. The model, which was called "The City of the World," was a utopian vision of humanity, "a place where the past and future come together, where good finally triumphs over evil....It's an imaginary place, but it's also realistic. Evil still exists, but the powers who rule over the city have figured out how to transform that evil back into good. Wisdom reigns here, but the struggle is nevertheless constant, and great vigilance is required of all the citizens — each of whom carries the entire city within himself."

The Sabbath is the Jewish scale model of ideal reality. It is a utopian vision, a day in which "the real world" is shut out, if only temporarily. It strengthens and inspires us to make the world into something that more closely resembles that scale model of the spirit. As the Zionist thinker Achad Ha Am wrote: "More than Israel has kept the Sabbath has the Sabbath kept Israel." In large measure, the Sabbath made the Jews a distinct people because it reminded them what the entire spectrum of Jewish living aimed to accomplish. It is a weekly preview of the Messianic Age.

Why did Jewish civilization produce the Sabbath?

Every unit of time — the day, the month, the year — is astronomically determined. Every unit, that is, except one. In *The Seven Day Circle: The History and Meaning of the Week,* Iranian-Jewish scholar Eviatar Zerubavel teaches that different cultures have different conceptualizations about the length of a week (which is, after all, an artificial, culturally determined creation). It could be two days, four days, ten days. In the West, a week lasts for seven days, mostly because God created for six days and rested on the seventh.

The Sabbath was intended to evoke a sense of *cosmic* rest, to embody an incredible paradox: God, more powerful than anything in the universe, *also* rested. In fact, the first thing that humans experienced of the world was God's rest, since the Eternal One ceased working the day after creating the first human. As the Sabbath liturgy suggests, by resting, God, the soul of the universe, *vayinafash,* "became endowed with a new soul." The Sabbath should be no less for us: Rest, replenishment and re-souling.

Which leads to the second aspect of the Sabbath: We rest

on the Sabbath not only to imitate God's rest, but to respond to the historical experience of the Jewish people. We rest as a *zecher l'yitziat Mitzrayim,* a memory of the Exodus from Egypt, as a way to remember our freedom from slavery. God created us to be free of the things that chain us to the world of working, having, owning and manipulating.

But while many modern Jews like the *idea* and the appeal of the Sabbath, they resist the *reality* of actually observing it. Once, we had sacred time. Now, we have Filofax. And in that journey of the spirit, we have become Sabbath-phobic.

That phobia is built into the very premise of Western civilization. The Roman philosopher Seneca, for example, complained that "to spend every seventh day without doing anything means to lose a seventh part of one's life." This is the classic criticism of the Sabbath: It is inefficient, which is similar to why many modern Jews don't sit *shiva* for a full seven days after a death. *Shiva* is "inefficient." And what is "useless" and "non-productive" frightens us.

Aristotle believed that the sole purpose of rest was to be able to work again: "We need relaxation because we cannot work continuously. Relaxation is not an end, for it is taken for the sake of activity." Aristotle didn't understand that leisure should have intrinsic meaning and importance and *not* just help us re-charge our engines for the next bout with the world.

Jump with me across the centuries from the ancient pagan criticisms of the Sabbath to our great-grandparents, who came as immigrants to America. Poor and stressed, they lived tenuous existences. Many were tailors and wagonmasters and shoemakers and barkeepers and middle-men — and they longed for the blessed rest of the Sabbath.

But many impoverished workers who emigrated to America left the idea of the Sabbath back home. Upon landing here, they encountered two ideologies that agreed on the importance of work: Socialism, which exalted the worker; and capitalism which venerated hard work. In their new world, the Sabbath was incongruous with the all-consuming work ethos.

The Depression reinforced the modern American obsession with work. Not to work was financially disastrous and psychologically traumatic. (It still is. Therapists note that for men, unemployment is often linked with sexual impotence.)

As anti-Semitism waned after World War Two, corporate barriers began to fall and Jews entered professions previously closed to them. Sabbath observance drastically declined since to celebrate a day of liberation from profession or career, after such a long fight to get that career, was almost unthinkable.

Earlier generations of Jews observed the Sabbath because it was what God wanted them to do. Later generations neglected it, except as nostalgia or ethnic memory. But there was never a time in American culture when the Sabbath was needed more than now. Many people want to break their bondage to career and materialism, yet don't know how to since modernity doesn't provide many models for that struggle. Judaism does — at least for one day.

The Sabbath is more than an obligation, more than candles, wine and religious services. It needs to be reframed so it can be what it was intended to be: A 24-hour protest against materialism, careerism and competition. In his essay entitled "Shabbat as Protest," Canadian Reform Rabbi W. Gunther Plaut wrote, "We must understand that doing nothing, being silent and open to the world, letting things happen inside, can be as important as — and sometimes more important than — what we commonly call 'useful'." The Sabbath is the ultimate statement that the world does not own us.

Consider how Blu Greenberg, an Orthodox Jewish feminist, re-states the Biblical commandment to rest on the seventh day:*

> "Six days shall you be a workaholic; on the seventh day, shall you join the serene company of human beings.
>
> "Six days shall you take orders from your boss; on the seventh day, shall you be master/mistress of your own life.
>
> "Six days shall you toil in the market; on the seventh day, shall you detach from money matters.
>
> "Six days shall you create, drive, invent, push; on the seventh day, shall you reflect.
>
> "Six days shall you be the perfect success; on the seventh day, shall you remember that not everything is in your power.
>
> "Six days shall you be a miserable failure; on the seventh day, shall you be on top of the world.
>
> *"Six days shall you enjoy the blessings of work; on the seventh day, shall you understand that being is as important as doing."*

The Sabbath teaches us that once a week, we can stop being doctors, dentists, salespeople, lawyers and we can be who

* *How to Run a Traditional Jewish Household,* c. 1993 by Blu Greenberg. Reprinted by permission of Simon & Schuster, Inc.

we really are. On the Sabbath, Jews remember that they have souls and depth, that they can speak to the universe and that the universe can speak back.

III. Pray daily

My friend in the wholesale food business once told me that he was thinking about turning a large, unused space in his factory into an interdenominational chapel for his employees. He hoped that this would spiritually invigorate them — and, in addition, reduce burnout and increase productivity.

This is a radical idea. A place for personal prayer in a place of business begins the task of sanctifying the profane. For what, we often think, could be more profane than the workplace? To attempt to meld work and worship with a chapel is to begin re-connecting the two meanings of the Hebrew term *avodah:* "work" and "worship."

If my friend ever does build his chapel, it will surely be the only one in a wholesale food firm in the entire country. No doubt it will be a boon to him and his co-workers and will brace them spiritually. Maybe it will even boost productivity. But, since few of us have such enlightened employers, the best we can do on a daily basis is to pray on our own or in a morning prayer group.

Yet, many contemporary Reform and Conservative Jews have a bias against personal, daily prayer. They associate it with an Orthodoxy that is alien to them. But relegating personal prayer to the exclusive province of certain Jews throws out a very valuable spiritual baby with a cultural bathwater.

Just as in the Middle Ages many Jewish theologian-physicians wrote prayers and meditations, so, too, now we need new prayers for professionals and workers, prayers that can help focus them on the day ahead, that can help them give thanks to God for what they have and ask God's help and support in times of crisis and challenge. Such prayers help us know that we serve something higher than ourselves, our egos, our colleagues, or our customers.

IV. Don't define yourself by your job or career

God made a covenant with every Jew, regardless of their economic status. As Deuteronomy 29:9-10 states, "You stand this day, *all of you* [italics added], before the Eternal your God...from woodchopper to waterdrawer — to enter into the covenant of the Eternal your God."

Thus, Judaism rejects the idea of a hierarchy of professions. The manual laborer has as much dignity as the physician. Work is a necessity for human existence, but not the center of it. As Reform Rabbi Dow Marmur wrote, "It is only those who live to work, rather than work to live, who are snobbish or status-seeking about their jobs."

The Midrash reminds us that God's test for a future leader is how he or she tends sheep. God saw Moses chase after a lamb that had separated from the flock. He saw the lamb drink from a spring of water, and he said, "If only I knew that you were thirsty I would have given you water to drink!" God saw that Moses knew how to keep track of the flock. At that moment, God knew that Moses was the right person to lead the Israelites out of Egypt and through the challenges of the wilderness.

Hasidism, which began in the 18th century as a spiritual revolution against the then-stultifying world of Talmudic learning, sanctified the work of common people. In one Hasidic tale, a man was rebuked for wearing a *tallit* and *tefillin* while repairing his wagon. "Look, he oils the wheels while he prays!" his neighbors taunted. "No," scolded their teacher, "he *prays* while he oils the wheels. Even in the midst of work, we focus our minds and souls on the higher things. What a holy people we are!" In another Hasidic story, a disciple travelled for miles to visit his teacher, Dov Baer of Mezeritch. He just wanted to see how the sage put on his shoes and tied his shoelaces. To Hasidim, everything is potentially useable in this world. No wisdom goes to waste.

I believe this is true. Waiters have taught me to find joy in serving people. Barbers tell me that they derive great pleasure from helping people look better and feel better. And cab drivers, of course, always have something to say, *if* you listen.

A few years ago, a young taxi driver drove me to John F. Kennedy Airport on Long Island. After a few minutes of conversation, I discovered that Mike had belonged to my synagogue years before I came to the community.

"So, rabbi," he asked while we sat in heavy traffic, "what do you say to a Jew like me who hasn't been in a synagogue since his bar mitzvah ceremony?"

Thinking for a moment, I recalled that in Hasidic lore, the *baal agalah* (the wagon driver) is an honored profession. So I said, "We could talk about your work."

"What does my work have to do with religion?"

"Well, we choose how we look at the world and at life. You're a taxi driver. But you are also a piece of the tissue that connects all humanity. You're taking me to the airport. I'll go to a different city and give a couple of lectures that might touch or help or change someone. I couldn't have gotten there without you. You help make that connection happen.

"I heard on your two-way radio that after you drop me off, you're going to pick up a woman from the hospital and take her home. That means that you'll be the first non-medical person she encounters after being in a hospital. You will be a small part of her healing process, an agent in her re-entry into the world of health.

"You may then pick up someone from the train station who has come home from seeing a dying parent. You may take someone to the house of the one that he or she will ask to join in marriage. You're a connector, a bridge builder. You're one of the unseen people who make the world work as well as it does. That is holy work. You may not think of it this way, but yours is a sacred mission."

The "simplest" professions can be metaphors for all human existence. To God, nothing is wasted. Every kind of gainful work can make us better people. As the second century sage Ben Azzai said in *Pirke Avot,* the ethical section of the Mishnah: "Treat no one lightly and think nothing is useless, for everyone has a moment and everything has its place."

V. Accept failure on the path to success

The chaplain in a Jewish geriatric center once told me that after years of working with the elderly, she had learned some invaluable lessons about the meaning of life and career.

"When I hear my clients' life stories," she said, "I have the enormous gift of hearing how life really plays itself out. I now realize that there is no such thing as a guaranteed upward career path. Career and profession do not always follow a straight line. Sometimes it's crooked, sometimes it's angular, sometimes it has false starts, fitful stops and detours."

Stop judging yourself by your accomplishments, my colleague had learned. *Sometimes failure is part of the game plan.*

A story about non-Jewish saintliness that illuminates our inner task: While Mother Teresa helped those starving in Ethiopia's famine during the 1980s, people were dying on all sides.

"How can you tend to the sick and the dying," an interviewer asked, "knowing that you will not be successful with everyone?"

"We are not here to be *successful,*" she answered. "We are here to be *faithful.*"

All of us need to be faithful to a higher sense of ourselves, faithful to a long-term goal and vision. *Pirke Avot* puts it in a slightly different way: "It is not up to you to finish the work, but neither are you free to desist from starting it." All work is ultimately unfinished, but our efforts should never be half-hearted.

VI. Stop trying to be perfect

Most professionals believe they have to be *omniscient* and *omnipotent* in their work. Men are particularly vulnerable to this, especially lawyers, doctors, clergy or any professional to whom people entrust their lives.

Recognize the margin of error you can tolerate. It will be different for every profession. To a journalist, a typographical error is less catastrophic than, say, a landing gear error is to an airline pilot. No one wants to commit errors in his or her work, but in certain professions the price for perfectionism can be the suppression of creativity.

Only God is God. The rest of us are only human, and human is not so bad. As the Psalmist said, human is just a little lower than the angels.

VII. Accept limits and boundaries

Technology has let our work invade every aspect of our lives: The cellular phone, the laptop computer, voice mail, even fax machines in the car. They make private time collapse and private space shrink. They give us a work-world without limits and boundaries and this, in turn, gives us an inner life that's cramped and narrow.

Every worthy spiritual system believes in limits and boundaries.

When the Jews received the Torah at Sinai, there were boundaries around the base of the mountain beyond which the Israelites could not go. The Sabbath is a boundary in time. Judaism has *food* boundaries: Donuts are fine, at least if they're kosher, but not during Passover. Food is indispensable, but not during Yom Kippur. Judaism's sexual boundaries rule against incest and adultery.

Boundaries and limits speak against the omniscience or omnipotence to which each of us, secretly or not so secretly, aspires. And yet, as Rabbi Harold Schulweis suggests, a biblical name for God is Shaddai, whose name means *dai,* "You have done enough already." This is the God Who teaches that there are borders and boundaries and appropriate levels of aspiration, who taught that life cannot be the Tower of Babel, which was erected so its builders could achieve fame and immortality.

None of us can do everything, no matter how worthy or how important our goals may be. And none of us can *be* everything or take advantage of every business or professional opportunity that comes our way.

"How do we find God?" a sage asks in the Midrash. "Through good deeds and study of Torah. And how does God find *us?* Through love, respect, companionship...through the temporary lessening of one's daily commerce, through 'No' that is really 'No', through 'Yes' that is really 'Yes.'"

Learn which aspect of work requires a "yes," and which requires a "no," or a "not yet," or even, "Someday I would like to...." Create boundaries: Of time, of effort, of aspiration.

VIII. Make room for God in your success — Bring in a partner

You didn't get to where you are today without skill, luck, patience, fortitude, great colleagues and loyal customers and faithful clients. Invariably, we forget to credit the one force that is above and behind everything that we do and everyone with whom we come in contact: God.

In Deuteronomy 8, Moses told the Israelites that after their forty-year trek through the wilderness they were about to enter "a land where you may eat food without stint, where you will lack nothing."

"When you have eaten your fill," he said, "and have built fine houses to live in, and your herds and flocks have multiplied, and your silver and gold have increased, and everything you own has prospered, beware lest your heart grow haughty and you forget the Eternal your God....and you say to yourselves, 'My own power and the might of my hand have won this wealth for me.' Remember that it is the Eternal your God who gives you the power to get wealth, in fulfillment of the covenant that He made on oath with your fathers, as is still the case."

Even thousands of years ago, Moses knew that each of us is tempted by arrogance and selfishness, by vain assumptions that we are the sole progenitors of all that we do. The wisdom he spoke on the eve of his people's entry into Israel still rings true. Its credence and force have a place in every shop and office and boardroom in late-20th-century America, in every business deal and artistic endeavor, in every ride we take in the elevator that carries us to yet another work day or every time we sit down in the pickup truck in which we ride on our appointed rounds.

Like the people of ancient Israel, we have built fine houses and our silver and gold have multiplied. Undeniably, we have prospered in many ways. But the price of that prosperity is a poverty of the soul. It is time to be as rich internally as we are externally; to be as rooted in the divine as we are in the material; to know that, as Moses said, it is God who gives us the power to acquire wealth, and that it is God who also gives us sustenance, to Whom we owe obeisance and thanks — and Who we should remember gave us not just this day and its accomplishments, but all of them.

Making It Real in Your Life

- ***List three ways to reduce your stress, workaholism and careerism.***
- ***How can you break out of "yourself" and give something back to the world?***
- ***How can you make the Sabbath into something holy for you?***
- ***How can you give thanks to God for the successes God has given you?***
- ***How can you be God's partner tomorrow?***
  Name one thing you can do to take the first step on this path.

"Go and Learn"

Suggestions for Further Reading

The following list contains books on the general topic of spirituality and work. It provides resources for your own explorations of how religious life can influence and shape what you do every day.

Berman, Phillip L. *The Search for Meaning: Americans Talk About What They Believe and Why*. New York: Ballantine Books, 1990. Narratives about the search for spirituality in everyday life.

Bolles, Richard Nelson. *What Color Is Your Parachute? A Practical Manual for Job Hunters and Career-Changers*. Berkeley, Calif.: Ten Speed Press, 1993. Bolles, a former minister, brings keen spiritual insights to career-planning.

Borowitz, Eugene B. *Exploring Jewish Ethics: Papers on Covenantal Responsibility*. Detroit, Mich.: Wayne State University Press, 1990. Includes several important essays on business and personal ethics.

Brener, Anne. *Mourning & Mitzvah: A Guided Journal for Walking the Mourner's Path Through Grief to Healing.* Woodstock, Vt.: Jewish Lights Publishing, 1993. Contains exercises to help people walk "through the valley of the shadow of death." Valuable for funeral directors and those who deal with grief.

Brooks, Andree Relion. *Children of Fast-Track Parents: Raising Self-Sufficient and Confident Children in an Achievement-Oriented World.* New York: Penguin, 1989. An articulate warning about how workaholism and careerism affect family life.

Business Ethics magazine. Edited by Marjorie Kelly. Published bimonthly by Mavis Publications, Inc., 52 S. 10th Street, #110, Minneapolis, MN. 55403-2001. (612) 962-4700. Deals exclusively with business ethics and the spiritual transformation of corporate life.

Carter, Stephen L. *The Culture of Disbelief: How American Law and Politics Trivialize Religious Devotion.* New York: Basic Books, 1993. On bringing religion into the public square and into our private lives.

Cowan, John. *The Common Table: Reflections and Meditations on Community and Spirituality in the Workplace.* New York: HarperCollins, 1993. Wistful meditations on work and meaning.

Dosick, Wayne. *The Business Bible: Ten New Commandments for Creating An Ethical Workplace.* New York: William Morrow, 1993. Reflections on how Jewish ethics and spirituality can improve the workplace.

Dossey, Larry. *Healing Words: The Power of Prayer and the Practice of Medicine.* New York: Harper San Francisco, 1993. How prayer sometimes "works" in the act of healing. Crucial to the spirituality of those in the healing profession.

Ehrenreich, Barbara. *Fear of Falling: The Inner Life of the Middle Class.* New York: Pantheon Books, 1989.

______. *The Worst Years of Our Lives: Irreverent Notes from a Decade Of Greed.* New York: Pantheon Books, 1990. Ehrenreich critiques how economic striving and frustration can wound the soul and the psyche.

Fassel, Diane. *Working Ourselves To Death: The High Cost of Workaholism and the Rewards of Recovery.* New York: HarperCollins, 1990. A most important contemporary book on the dangers of workaholism.

Freudenberger, Herbert J. with Geraldine Richelson. *Burn Out: How To Beat the High Cost of Success.* New York: Doubleday, 1980. A warning to all of us.

Gaylin, Willard. *Adam and Eve and Pinocchio: On Being and Becoming Human.* New York: Viking, 1990. A meditation on human nature, including the meaning of work in a post-Garden of Eden world.

Green, Arthur. *Seek My Face, Speak My Name: A Contemporary Jewish Theology.* Northvale, N.J.: Jason Aronson, 1992. A re-constructed Jewish theology for our time.

Greenberg, Blu. *How To Run A Traditional Jewish Household.* New York: Simon and Schuster, 1989. Shows how a traditional Jewish life style, with its heavy emphasis on Shabbat, can be spiritually redemptive.

Greenberg, Irving. *The Jewish Way: Living the Holidays.* New York: Summit, 1988. In particular, see the chapter on Shabbat.

Heinze, Andrew R. *Adapting to Abundance: Jewish Immigrants, Mass Consumption, and the Search for American Identity.* New York: Columbia University Press, 1990. How American Jews acculturated to material prosperity. A wonderful social history.

Hertzberg, Arthur. *The Jews in America.* New York: Simon and Schuster, 1989. A critical view of American Jewish history. Contends that Eastern European Jews came to America more for economic reasons than for religious freedom.

Heschel, Abraham J. *The Sabbath: Its Meaning for Modern Man.* New York: Farrar, Straus, and Giroux, 1951. The classic statement on the meaning of spiritual rest for moderns.

Kellner, Menachem Marc, ed. *Contemporary Jewish Ethics.* New York: Sanhedrin Press, 1978. Important essays on medical and business ethics.

Lasch, Christopher. *The True and Only Heaven: Progress and Its Critics.* New York: W.W. Norton and Company, 1991. Excellent critique of *laissez-faire* consumer capitalism.

McCormack, Mark H. *What They Don't Teach You At Harvard Business School: Notes From a Street-Smart Executive.* New York: Bantam Books, 1984. More than simply "How To Get Ahead." Forces us to evaluate our inner lives.

Meier, Levi, ed. *Jewish Values in Psychotherapy: Essays on Vital Issues on the Search for Meaning.* Lanham, Md.: University Press of America, 1988. The interplay between traditional Jewish belief and psychotherapy.

____, ed. *Jewish Values in Health And Medicine.* Lanham, Md.: University Press of America, 1991. Excellent essays on the nature of illness and healing.

Novak, David. *Jewish Social Ethics.* New York: Oxford University Press, 1992. Essays on economic, medical, and technological ethics. Applicable to many professions.

Roof, Wade Clark. *A Generation of Seekers: The Spiritual Journeys of the Baby Boom Generation.* New York: HarperCollins, 1993. The spiritual angst of our time, addressed with wisdom.

Saltzman, Amy. *Downshifting: Reinventing Success On A Slower Track.* New York: HarperCollins, 1992. How to get off the fast track. Includes concrete examples of those who did it.

Schmookler, Andrew Bard. *Fool's Gold: The Fate of Values in a World of Goods.* New York: HarperCollins, 1993. Superb critique of materialism.

Schor, Juliet B. *The Overworked American: The Unexpected Decline of Leisure.* New York: Basic Books, 1993. The sociological perspective on overworking.

Shapiro, Mark Dov, ed. *Gates of Shabbat: A Guide for Observing Shabbat.* New York: Central Conference of American Rabbis, 1991. Once you decide that you want to observe Shabbat, how to do it "right" (for liberal Jews).

Tamari, Meir. *"With All Your Possessions": Jewish Ethics and Economic Life.* New York: Free Press, 1987. Definitive book on Jewish business ethics and economic theory.

About JEWISH LIGHTS Publishing

People of all faiths and backgrounds yearn for books that attract, engage, educate and spiritually inspire.

Our principal goal is to stimulate thought and help all people learn about who the Jewish People are, where they come from, and what the future can be made to hold. While people of our diverse Jewish heritage are the primary audience, our books speak to the Christian world as well and will broaden their understanding of Judaism and the roots of their own faith.

We bring to you authors who are at the forefront of spiritual thought and experience. While each has something different to say, they all say it in a voice that you can hear.

Our books are designed to welcome you and then to engage, stimulate and inspire. We judge our success not only by whether or not our books are beautiful and commercially successful, but by whether or not they make a difference in your life.

We at Jewish Lights take great care to produce beautiful books that present meaningful spiritual content in a form that reflects the art of making high quality books. Therefore, we want to acknowledge those who contributed to the production of this book.

PRODUCTION
Wendy Kilborn

EDITORIAL & PROOFREADING
Sandra Korinchak

BOOK & COVER DESIGN
Glenn Suokko, Woodstock, Vermont

TYPE
Set in Baskerville
Glenn Suokko, Woodstock, Vermont

COVER PRINTING
Phoenix Color, Long Island City, New York

PRINTING AND BINDING
Book Press, Brattleboro, Vermont

Bring Spirituality into Your Daily Life

BEING GOD'S PARTNER

How to Find the Hidden Link Between Spirituality and Your Work

by *Dr. Jeffrey K. Salkin*
Introduction by *Norman Lear*

How to Find the Hidden Link Between Spirituality and Your Work

by Dr. Jeffrey K. Salkin
Introduction by Norman Lear

A book that will challenge people of every denomination to reconcile the cares of work and soul. A groundbreaking book about spirituality and the work world, from a Jewish perspective. Helps the reader find God in the ethical striving and search for meaning in the professions and in business. Critiques our modern culture of workaholism and careerism, and offers practical suggestions for balancing your professional life and spiritual self.

Being God's Partner will inspire people of all faiths and no faith to find greater meaning in their work, and see themselves doing God's work in the world.

"His is an eloquent voice, bearing an important and concrete message of authentic Jewish religion. The book is engaging, easy to read and hard to put down — and it will make a difference and change people."

— Jacob Neusner, Distinguished Research Professor of Religious Studies, University of South Florida, author of *The Doubleday Anchor Reference Library Introduction to Rabbinic Literature*

6" x 9", 175 pp. (est.) Hardcover, ISBN 1-879045-37-0 **$19.95**

Available: October '94

SELF, STRUGGLE & CHANGE

Family Conflict Stories in Genesis and their Insights for Our Lives

by *Dr. Norman J. Cohen*

How do I find greater wholeness in my life and in my family's life?

The stress of late-20th-century living only brings new variations to timeless personal struggles. The people described by the biblical writers of Genesis were in situations and relationships very much like our own. We identify with them. Their stories still speak to us because they are about the same problems we deal with every day.

A modern master of biblical interpretation brings us greater understanding of the ancient text and of ourselves in this intriguing re-telling of conflict between husband and wife, father and son, brothers, and sisters.

6" x 9", 200 pp. (est.) Hardcover, ISBN 1-879045-19-2 **$21.95** (est.)

Available: November '94

SO THAT YOUR VALUES LIVE ON

Ethical Wills & How To Prepare Them

Edited by *Rabbi Jack Riemer & Professor Nathaniel Stampfer*

So that your values live on-Ethical Wills and how to prepare them

A cherished Jewish tradition, ethical wills—parents writing to children or grandparents to grandchildren—sum up what people have learned and express what they want most for, and from, their loved ones. Includes an intensive guide, **"How to Write Your Own Ethical Will,"** and a topical index. A marvelous treasury of wills: Herzl, Sholom Aleichem, Israelis, Holocaust victims, contemporary American Jews.

"This remarkable volume will enrich all those who will read it and meditate upon its infinite wisdom." — *Elie Wiesel*

6"x 9", 272 pp. Quality Paperback, ISBN 1-879045-34-6 **$16.95** HC, ISBN -07-9 **$23.95**

Spiritual Inspiration for Family Life

IN GOD'S NAME

by Sandy Sasso

Illus. by Phoebe Stone

IN GOD'S NAME

For children K-5

by *Sandy Eisenberg Sasso*
Full color illustrations by *Phoebe Stone*

Like an ancient myth in its poetic text and vibrant illustrations, this modern fable about the search for God's name celebrates the diversity and, at the same time, the unity of all the people of the world. Each seeker claims he or she alone knows the answer. Finally, they come together and learn what God's name really is, sharing the ultimate harmony of belief in one God by people of all faiths, all backgrounds.

"I got goosebumps when I read *In God's Name,* its language and illustrations are that moving. This is a book children will love and the whole family will cherish for its beauty and power."
—*Francine Klagsbrun,* author of *Mixed Feelings: Love, Hate, Rivalry, and Reconciliation Among Brothers and Sisters*

9" x 12", 32 pp. Hardcover, Full color illus., ISBN 1-879045-26-5 **$16.95**

GOD'S PAINTBRUSH

by *Sandy Eisenberg Sasso*
Full color illustrations by *Annette Compton*

• AWARD WINNER •

MULTICULTURAL, NON-SECTARIAN, NON-DENOMINATIONAL. Invites children of all faiths and backgrounds to encounter God openly in their own lives. Wonderfully interactive, provides questions adult and child can explore together at the end of each episode.

"The most exciting religious children's book I have seen in years."
—*Sylvia Avner, Children's Librarian, 92nd St. "Y," NYC*

"An excellent way to honor the imaginative breadth and depth of the spiritual life of the young." —*Dr. Robert Coles, Harvard University*

For children K–4 elementary

11"x 8½", 32 pp. Hardcover, Full color illustrations, ISBN 1-879045-22-2 **$15.95**

The NEW Jewish Baby BOOK
Names, Ceremonies & Customs
A Guide for Today's Families
RITUALS Traditions & Choices
CELEBRATIONS To Welcome Daughter & Son
NAMES A Unique Directory
INTERFAITH FAMILIES Ideas & Information
ANITA DIAMANT
Foreword by Rabbi Norman J. Cohen
Preface by Rabbi Amy Eilberg

THE *NEW* JEWISH BABY BOOK

Names, Ceremonies, Customs — A Guide for Today's Families

by *Anita Diamant*
Foreword by *Rabbi Norman J. Cohen, Dean, HUC–JIR, NYC*
Introduction by *Rabbi Amy Eilberg*

A complete guide to the customs and rituals for welcoming a new child to the world and into the Jewish community, and for commemorating this joyous event in family life–whatever your family constellation. Updated, revised and expanded edition of the highly acclaimed *The Jewish Baby Book*. Includes new ceremonies for girls, celebrations in interfaith families. Also contains a unique directory of names that reflects the rich diversity of the Jewish experience.

"A book that all Jewish parents—no matter how religious—will find fascinating as well as useful. It is a perfect shower or new baby gift." — *Pamela Abrams, Exec. Editor,* Parents Magazine

6"x 9", 328 pp. Quality Paperback Original, ISBN 1-879045-28-1 **$15.95**

PUTTING GOD ON THE GUEST LIST

AWARD WINNER

How to Reclaim the Spiritual Meaning of Your Child's Bar or Bat Mitzvah

by *Rabbi Jeffrey K. Salkin*
Foreword by *Rabbi Sandy Eisenberg Sasso*
Introduction by *Rabbi William H. Lebeau, Vice Chancellor, JTS*

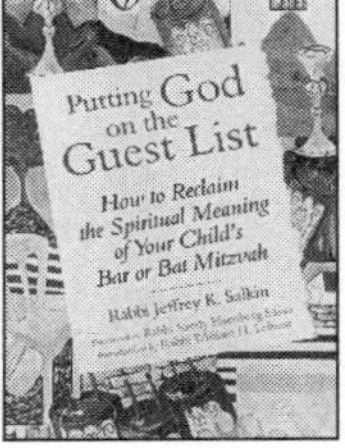

Joining explanation, instruction and inspiration, helps parent and child truly *be there* when the moment of Sinai is recreated in their lives. Asks and answers such fundamental questions as how did Bar and Bat Mitzvah originate? What is the lasting significance of the event? How to make the event more spiritually meaningful?

"Shows the way to restore spirituality and depth to every young Jew's most important rite of passage." — *Rabbi Joseph Telushkin, author of* Jewish Literacy

"I hope every family planning a Bar Mitzvah celebration reads Rabbi Salkin's book."
— *Rabbi Harold S. Kushner, author of* When Bad Things Happen to Good People

6"x 9", 184 pp. Quality Paperback, ISBN 1-879045-10-9 **$14.95** HC, ISBN -20-6 **$21.95**

Add Greater Meaning to Your Life

FAITH AFTER THE HOLOCAUST?

NEW!
in paperback
Avail. Sept. '94

AWARD WINNER **THE SPIRIT OF RENEWAL**

Finding Faith After the Holocaust
by *Edward Feld*

"Boldly redefines the landscape of Jewish religious thought after the Holocaust." — *Rabbi Lawrence Kushner*

Trying to understand the Holocaust and addressing the question of faith after the Holocaust, Rabbi Feld explores three key cycles of destruction and recovery in Jewish history, each of which radically reshaped Jewish understanding of God, people, and the world.

"Undoubtedly the most moving book I have read....'Must' reading."
— *Rabbi Howard A. Addison*, Conservative Judaism

"A profound meditation on Jewish history [and the Holocaust]....Christians, as well as many others, need to share in this story." —*The Rt. Rev. Frederick H. Borsch, Ph.D., Episcopal Bishop of L.A.*

6"x 9", 216 pp. Hardcover, ISBN 1-879045-06-0 **$22.95**
6"x 9", 224 pp. Quality Paperback, ISBN 1-879045-40-0 **$16.95**

SEEKING THE PATH TO LIFE AWARD WINNER

Theological Meditations On God and the Nature of People, Love, Life and Death
by *Rabbi Ira F. Stone,*
Ornamentation by *Annie Stone*

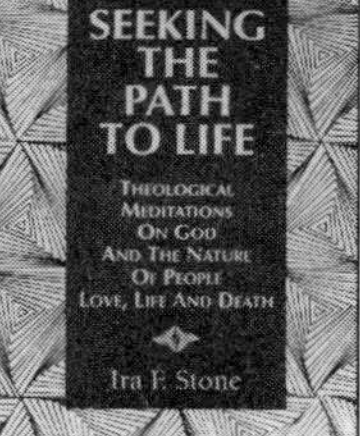

For people who never thought they would read a book of theology—let alone understand it, enjoy it, savor it and have it affect the way they think about their lives.

In 45 intense meditations, each a page or two in length, Stone takes us on explorations of the most basic human struggles: life and death, love and anger, peace and war, covenant and exile.

"Exhilarating—unlike any other reading that I have done in years."
—*Rabbi Neil Gillman, The Jewish Theological Seminary*

"A bold book....The reader of any faith will be inspired, challenged and led more deeply into their own encounter with God."
— *The Rev. Carla Berkedal, Episcopal Priest, Executive Director of Earth Ministry*

6"x 9", 144 pp. Hardcover, ISBN 1-879045-17-6 **$19.95**

THE EMPTY CHAIR: FINDING HOPE & JOY

Timeless Wisdom from a Hasidic Master, Rebbe Nachman of Breslov

Adapted by *Moshe Mykoff* and *the Breslov Research Institute*

A "little treasure" of aphorisms and advice for living joyously and spiritually today, written 200 years ago, but startlingly fresh in meaning and use. Challenges and helps us to move from stress and sadness to hope and joy.

Teacher, guide and spiritual master—Rebbe Nachman provides vital words of inspiration and wisdom for life today for people of any faith, or of no faith.

4" x 6", 128 pp. Hardcover, ISBN 1-879045-16-8 **$9.95**

Motivation & Inspiration for Recovery

TWELVE JEWISH STEPS TO RECOVERY

A Personal Guide To Turning From Alcoholism & Other Addictions...Drugs, Food, Gambling, Sex

by *Rabbi Kerry M. Olitzky* & *Stuart A. Copans, M.D.*
Preface by Abraham J. Twerski, M.D.
Introduction by Rabbi Sheldon Zimmerman
Illustrations by Maty Grünberg
"Getting Help" by JACS Foundation

A Jewish perspective on the Twelve Steps of addiction recovery programs with consolation, inspiration and motivation for recovery. It draws from traditional sources, and quotes from what recovering Jewish people say about their experiences with addictions of all kinds. Inspiring illustrations of the twelve gates of the Old City of Jerusalem.

Experts Praise *Twelve Jewish Steps to Recovery*

"Recommended reading for people of all denominations." — Rabbi Abraham J. Twerski, M.D.

"I read Twelve Jewish Steps with the eyes of a Christian and came away renewed in my heart. I felt like I had visited my Jewish roots. These authors have deep knowledge of recovery as viewed by Alcoholics Anonymous." — Rock J. Stack, M.A., L.L.D. Manager of Clinical/Pastoral Education, Hazelden Foundation

"This book is the first aimed directly at helping the addicted person and family. Everyone affected or interested should read it." — Sheila B. Blume, M.D., C.A.C., Medical Director, Alcoholism, Chemical Dependency and Compulsive Gambling Programs, South Oaks Hospital, Amityville, NY

Readers Praise *Twelve Jewish Steps to Recovery*

"A God-send. Literally. A book from the higher power." — New York, NY
"Looking forward to using it in my practice." —Michigan City, IN
"Made me feel as though 12 Steps were for me, too." — Long Beach, CA
"Excellent–changed my life." — Elkhart Lake, WI

6" x 9", 136 pp. Quality Paperback, ISBN 1-879045-09-5 **$12.95**

RECOVERY FROM Codependence

A Jewish Twelve Steps Guide to Healing Your Soul

by *Rabbi Kerry M. Olitzky*
Foreword by *Marc Galanter, M.D., Director, Division of Alcoholism & Drug Abuse, NYU Medical Center*
Afterword by *Harriet Rossetto, Director, Gateways Beit T'shuvah*

For the estimated 90% of America struggling with the addiction of a family member or loved one, or involved in a dysfunctional family or relationship. A follow-up to the ground-breaking *Twelve Jewish Steps to Recovery.*

"The disease of chemical dependency is also a family illness. Rabbi Olitzky offers spiritual hope and support." —*Jerry Spicer, President, Hazelden*

"Another major step forward in finding the sources and resources of healing, both physical and spiritual, in our tradition." —*Rabbi Sheldon Zimmerman, Temple Emanu-El, Dallas, TX*

6" x 9", 160 pp. Hardcover, ISBN 1-879045-27-3 **$21.95**
6" x 9", 160 pp. Quality Paperback, ISBN 1-879045-32-X **$13.95**

Motivation & Inspiration for Recovery

RENEWED EACH DAY

Daily Twelve Step Recovery Meditations Based on the Bible

by *Rabbi Kerry M. Olitzky* & *Aaron Z.*

VOLUME I: Genesis & Exodus
Introduction by *Rabbi Michael A. Signer*
Afterword by JACS Foundation

VOLUME II: Leviticus, Numbers & Deuteronomy
Introduction by *Sharon M. Strassfeld*
Afterword by *Rabbi Harold M. Schulweis*

Using a seven day/weekly guide format, a recovering person and a spiritual leader who is reaching out to addicted people reflect on the traditional weekly Bible reading. They bring strong spiritual support for daily living and recovery from addictions of all kinds: alcohol, drugs, eating, gambling and sex. A profound sense of the religious spirit soars through their words and brings all people in Twelve Step recovery programs home to a rich and spiritually enlightening tradition.

"Meets a vital need; it offers a chance for people turning from alcoholism and addiction to renew their spirits and draw upon the Jewish tradition to guide and enrich their lives."
—*Rabbi Irving (Yitz) Greenberg, President, CLAL, The National Jewish Center for Learning and Leadership*

"Will benefit anyone familiar with a 'religion of the Book.' Jews, Christians, Muslims. . . ."
—*Ernest Kurtz, author of* Not-God: A History of Alcoholics Anonymous & The Spirituality of Imperfection

"An enduring impact upon the faith community as it seeks to blend the wisdom of the ages represented in the tradition with the twelve steps to recovery and wholeness."
—*Robert H. Albers, Ph.D., Editor,* Journal of Ministry in Addiction & Recovery

Beautiful Two-Volume Set.

6"x 9", V. I, 224 pp. / V. II, 280 pp., Quality Paperback, ISBN 1-879045-21-4 **$27.90**

ONE HUNDRED BLESSINGS EVERY DAY

Daily Twelve Step Recovery Affirmations, Exercises for Personal Growth & Renewal Reflecting Seasons of the Jewish Year

by *Dr. Kerry M. Olitzky*
with selected meditations prepared by *Rabbi James Stone Goodman, Danny Siegel,* and *Rabbi Gordon Tucker*
Foreword by *Rabbi Neil Gillman, The Jewish Theological Seminary of America*
Afterword by *Dr. Jay Holder, Director, Exodus Treatment Center*

100 Blessings Every Day
Daily Twelve Step Recovery Affirmations, Exercises for Personal Growth & Renewal Reflecting Seasons of the Jewish Year
Rabbi Kerry M. Olitzky
Rabbi Neil Gillman, The Jewish Theological Seminary
Foreword Are The Twelve Steps Jewish?
Sir Jay M. Holder, D.C., M.D., Ph.D.
Afterword Spiritual Renewal in the Jewish Calendar

Recovery is a conscious choice from moment to moment, day in and day out. In this helpful and healing book of daily recovery meditations, Kerry Olitzky gives us words to live by day after day, throughout the annual cycle of holiday observances and special Sabbaths of the Jewish calendar.

For those facing the struggles of daily living, *One Hundred Blessings Every Day* brings solace and hope to anyone who is open to healing and to the recovery-oriented teachings that can be gleaned from the Bible and Jewish tradition.

4½" x 6½", Quality Paperback, 432 pp. ISBN 1-879045-30-3 **$14.95**

Spiritual Inspiration for Daily Living . . .

THE BOOK OF WORDS
Talking Spiritual Life, Living Spiritual Talk

by *Lawrence Kushner*

In the incomparable manner of his extraordinary *The Book of Letters: A Mystical Hebrew Alphabet,* Kushner now lifts up and shakes the dust off primary religious words we use to describe the spiritual dimension of life. The *Words* take on renewed spiritual significance, adding power and focus to the lives we live every day.

For each word Kushner offers us a startling, moving and insightful explication, and pointed readings from classical Jewish sources that further illuminate the concept. He concludes with a short exercise that helps unite the spirit of the word with our actions in the world.

6"x 9", 152 pp. Hardcover, two-color text ISBN 1-879045-35-4 **$21.95**

"It is wonderful! A surprise at every page. His translations and elaborations provoke and stimulate the religious imagination." —*Rabbi Neil Gillman, Chair, Dept. of Jewish Philosophy, Jewish Theological Seminary*

"Breathes new life into a vocabulary that many may have thought to be irrelevant or outdated. Kushner is one of the great spiritual teachers of our time. He once again succeeds in offering us wisdom and inspiration."

—*Ellen Umansky, co-editor,* Four Centuries of Jewish Women's Spirituality: A Sourcebook

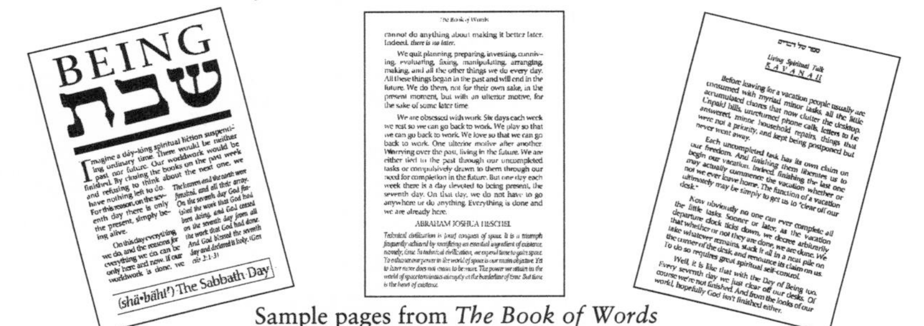

BEING שבת

Imagine a day-long spiritual fiction suspending ordinary time. There would be neither past nor future. Our worldwork would be finished. By closing the books on the past week and refusing to think about the next one, we have nothing left to do. For this reason, on the seventh day there is only the present, simply being alive.

On this day everything we do, and the reasons for everything we do, can be only here and now. If our worldwork is done, we

The heaven and the earth were finished, and all their array. On the seventh day God finished the work that God had been doing, and God ceased on the seventh day from all the work that God had done. And God blessed the seventh day and declared it holy. (Genesis 2:1-3)

(shä•bäht') The Sabbath Day

cannot do anything about making it better later. Indeed, *there is no later.*

We quit planning, preparing, investing, conniving, evaluating, fixing, manipulating, arranging, making, and all the other things we do every day. All these things began in the past and will end in the future. We do them, not for their own sake, in the present moment, but with an ulterior motive, for the sake of some later time.

We are obsessed with work. Six days each week we rest so we can go back to work. We play so that we can go back to work. We love so that we can go back to work. One ulterior motive after another. Worrying over the past, living in the future. We are either tied to the past through our uncompleted tasks or compulsively drawn to them through our need for completion in the future. But one day each week there is a day devoted to being present, the seventh day. On that day, we do not have to go anywhere or do anything. Everything is done and we are already here.

ABRAHAM JOSHUA HESCHEL

Sample pages from *The Book of Words*

AWARD WINNER

THE BOOK OF LETTERS
A Mystical Hebrew Alphabet

by *Rabbi Lawrence Kushner*

In calligraphy by the author. Folktales about and exploration of the mystical meanings of the Hebrew Alphabet. Open the old prayerbook-like pages of *The Book of Letters* and you will enter a special world of sacred tradition and religious feeling. More than just symbols, all twenty-two letters of the Hebrew alphabet overflow with meanings and personalities of their own.

Rabbi Kushner draws from ancient Judaic sources, weaving Talmudic commentary, Hasidic folktales, and Kabbalistic mysteries around the letters.

"A book which is in love with Jewish letters." — Isaac Bashevis Singer (ז"ל)

• Popular Hardcover Edition
6"x 9", 80 pp. Hardcover, two colors, inspiring new Foreword.
ISBN 1-879045-00-1 **$24.95**

• Deluxe Gift Edition
9"x 12", 80 pp. Hardcover, four-color text, ornamentation, in a beautiful slipcase.
ISBN 1-879045-01-X **$79.95**

• Collector's Limited Edition
9"x 12", 80 pp. Hardcover, gold embossed pages, hand assembled slipcase. With silkscreened print.

Limited to 500 signed and numbered copies.

ISBN 1-879045-04-4 **$349.00**

To see a sample page at no obligation, call us

. . . .The Kushner Series

GOD WAS IN THIS PLACE & I, i DID NOT KNOW

Finding Self, Spirituality & Ultimate Meaning

by *Lawrence Kushner*

Who am I? Who is God? Kushner creates inspiring interpretations of Jacob's dream in Genesis, opening a window into Jewish spirituality for people of all faiths and backgrounds.

In a fascinating blend of scholarship, imagination, psychology and history, seven Jewish spiritual masters ask and answer fundamental questions of human experience.

"A brilliant fabric of classic rabbinic interpretations, Hasidic insights and literary criticism which warms us and sustains us."

—*Dr. Norman J. Cohen, Dean, Hebrew Union College, NY*

"Rich and intriguing." —*M. Scott Peck, M.D., author of* The Road Less Traveled

6"x 9", 192 pp. Hardcover, ISBN 1-879045-05-2 **$21.95**
6"x 9", 192 pp. Quality Paperback, ISBN 1-879045-33-8 **$16.95**

HONEY FROM THE ROCK

An Introduction to Jewish Mysticism

by *Lawrence Kushner*

An introduction to the ten gates of Jewish mysticism and how it applies to daily life.

"Quite simply the easiest introduction to Jewish mysticism you can read."

"*Honey from the Rock* captures the flavor and spark of Jewish mysticism. . . . Read it and be rewarded." —*Elie Wiesel*

"A work of love, lyrical beauty, and prophetic insight. "
—*Father Malcolm Boyd,* The Christian Century

6"x 9", 168 pp. Quality Paperback, ISBN 1-879045-02-8 **$14.95**

THE RIVER OF LIGHT

Spirituality, Judaism, Consciousness

by *Lawrence Kushner*

A "manual" for all spiritual travelers who would attempt a spiritual journey in our times. Taking us step by step, Kushner allows us to discover the meaning of our own quest: "to allow the river of light—the deepest currents of consciousness—to rise to the surface and animate our lives."

"Philosophy and mystical fantasy...exhilarating speculative flights launched from the Bible....Anybody—Jewish, Christian, or otherwise...will find this book an intriguing experience."—The Kirkus Reviews

"A very important book."—*Rabbi Adin Steinsaltz*

6"x 9", 180 pp. Quality Paperback, ISBN 1-879045-03-6 **$14.95**